THE GRAY BOOK

MERIDIAN

Crossing Aesthetics

Werner Hamacher
& David E. Wellbery
Editors

*Stanford
University
Press*

*Stanford
California
1999*

THE GRAY BOOK

Aris Fioretos

An earlier version of *The Gray Book*
was published in Swedish in 1994
by Norstedts Förlag AB, Stockholm,
as *Den grå boken*. © Aris Fioretos, 1994

Stanford University Press
Stanford, California

© 1999 by the Board of Trustees of the
Leland Stanford Junior University

Printed in the United States of America

CIP data appear at the end of the book

For William Gass

grau, theurer Freund, ist alle Theorie
—Goethe

Contents

The Gray Book   1

Acknowledgments   151

Gray and falling, and while falling waiting for the strange moment when the tongue turns light and limber, liquid with avowal, the teeth become dragons, and the instant suddenly resembles the drowner's last dream, he who fell from a precipice and now sinks like a stone but lackadaisically as a leaf, winging swinging like a dim dot suspended in motion, yet moving toward rest because the present's elastic membrane has placidly expanded, now permitting images of past and prior to pour into appearance as he sinks glides sinks downward inside its roomy pocket in a dissident sort of rhythm —another cadence, another clause, another clue—contained in a depth that is its own surface encasement . . . and it is at that moment, comfortably cushioned yet malleable, when we have closed our eyes, resting on a mattress perhaps, or a cot, that it all begins . . . gradually the well-known surroundings disappear, although we still seem to perceive the table's flat surface in front of us or the flower-patterned fringed bedspread covering our dishevelled body in the manner of a rippled ocean out of which peaks and summits emerge like distending formations in a mist-distorted land. After a while, however, the familiar particulars blend, blur, and concoct as they are being transformed into a two-dimensional space that expands lingeringly and lazily, slightly tilted toward our eyes . . . still hovering longingly . . . but lacking the intimacy of earlier impressions. At first it seems vague, this spacious flatness, or rather neutral, without shape and color, but soon it appears to possess at least two qualities: it becomes more or less dark depending on how hard we close our eyes, as if the weight with which it leans against them depended on how forcefully we allow it to roll and rock the eyelids against their viscous pellets; next, it appears irregular and the distribution of darkness thus must be uneven. The upper part, for example, is noticeably lighter, although it seems to withdraw and level out in an upward direction, while the lower, which ought to lie closer (but notions of nearness and distance, up and down, do not seem applicable here) is, for one, much more obscure, that is, not neutral as we first thought, but, in fact, blacker shoddier downright dark, and, for another, seems to thicken to such compactness that it is impossible to determine whether it ceases or rather loses itself in a wide woolly void. The more we focus on this downy density, the more we notice how it moves, glides, or rather floats, and after a while we are convinced that whatever it is, it is not exactly solid, but consists of innumerable layers closely compressed and folded, like once-upon-a-time napkins among lavender in drawers of oak. We observe them from where we are, slightly above and across, and without moving we examine their consistency, as duplicitous as smooth sheets of snowfall. We cannot touch these layers, of course, despite being so close, yet we understand that they would scatter, most likely, if we touched them, and we think we know they are not made of near-mute matter, muffled like words spoken under heavy blankets, but rather of strings of dusty powder as airy yet tight as our breath under such strenuous circumstances. Soft arrays of cloudiness, weighted with languor and abandon. After sinking for a while, we realize we are in the process of falling asleep and that the thick thud with which vapor is wrapping us must be sleep itself that has arrived. Finally. Yet . . . Wait. Hold it. Just this: in order to be embraced by such feathery fold, descending like slow tender fog, it is not enough to be ready, tucked away like a knife under a pillow, but an action is required that, however, demands passiveness more than activity, and while it appears to be simplicity itself, we believe it will prove exacting. Not only does it require us to reduce the body to a point without extension, like an empty pupil contracting nil but not being null, at the same time it turns the two-dimensional space in front of us into a vaulted enclosure. A gaseous envelope containing the swarthy silence of rain. Or a cobwebby palm casually clasping and cautiously closing. There. And while we are falling, and falling waiting for the moment when we shall pass over the threshold without being aware of it, finally embraced by amity and placidness, we begin to make out the images hovovering around us.

"Real comfort," holds the author of *A Day Book*, amounts to such "moments before sleep," but "also, just at wakening. A gray-like warmth," and he dates the entry "February 6." In the beginning, as in our case, there might be one or two restless moves of limb and some feeble attempt at resurrection (done mainly for the record), later a brief turn to the top perhaps, then a longer to the bottom, but once we have made these measurements of a bodily arrangement we are in no position to query, we find ourselves in sleep's downy embrace. Remaining residues of anatomical discomfort are absorbed by delicate folds of enchanting calm—and we realize that, indeed, surrender may make for ingenious joy. Besides, to ease the transition, there is that lax warmth, so soothing in its nondescript way. "Gray-like" might be just the right word for it. In any event, according to Robert Creeley, this odd heat clears a liminal zone (crossing, shadow, passage) that despite the haphazard character of the situation provides comfort. In a sense, that is, safety may be found in transitory states. We would do well to remember that. In its own momentary manner, *A Day Book* proposes a thesis on threshold living.

Let us examine this proposition concerning transient existence, let us hold its rustling evanescence in a hand we shall have to produce for the occasion . . . rub, scrub . . . fingers . . . five . . . there: it vanishes! And so transience must come as it goes—must it not?—emerging only as disappearance. Now here, now not. Now there and not. What an odd thing: like a person falling asleep, that which is "gray-like" seems part of its own absence. But in that case, what *will* last? For us, we suspect, only this: our empty hand, hastily conjured forth, but tranquilly kept. Or also: these fingers, haphazardly invoked and then longingly closing on a specimen of nothing. Much like sleep's soft grasp. Precisely. And this, we promise, shall be our single concern, our sole abode: the threshold region the hand may gather for us to envision when we no longer see, tenderly drawing this lively pattern, that reluctant design, in which everything emerges fadingly . . . is contrived as it vanishes . . . and inflated and exhaled. Being without being. O. Figures of dust. Yes. And their incomparable effects.

We may try, of course, to record more properly an existence as it might be lived in this volatile domain, as wobbly as a subjunctive. Perhaps even present an exposé—convincingly contrived, naturally—that would bring order among the doings of its supposed proprietor, phantom-limbed *N. N.* Then we would be able to describe the ambiguity of atmosphere and abandon that, by accounting for assumptions concocted, conjectures made, might slowly set apart our own being from the object under scrutiny . . . and thus establish the distance needed for certainty. But would such a venture be believable? Difficult to tell, impossible to know. Still: not likely. There is no need to go on record here. No treatise is required, certainly no tract, and preferably no pamphlet (flitting in the none-too-innocent manner of a handkerchief caught in the flux of opinion). Also, why bother with inspection when there is projection? Perhaps a handful of personal reflections would suffice instead, thrown like quick glances into a mirror or launched like longing looks in the direction of recollections receding like currents of water down a drain . . . more or less empathizing attempts, that is, whose purpose is to feel for the twists and peculiarities of an imagined subject—these identificatory assumptions, so insubstantial in form, to which we are prone when given to sleep?

Yes, maybe . . . just possibly . . . but: no. It seems more than enough to remain in the suspended animation referred to as an "essay," freed from both detachment and empathy, the realm of doubt and questioning in which we find ourselves when we look neither for truth, supposedly neutral, nor for a show of idiosyncratic understanding, but rather for that "something" that lies in-between.

("A person who desires truth becomes a scholar," Robert Musil once remarked, "the person who wants to put his or her subjectivity into play becomes perhaps a writer; but what should he or she do who is looking for something in-between?") Because above all, we cherish the exercises of sensuous mindfulness, the lush labors of uncertainty—that strange activity, psychic and physical alike, in which it remains unclear if we discover or invent, receive or project meaning. For which purpose we may well stay where we are, in this gray-like warmth, neither properly objective, nor thoroughly subjective, practicing the art of attention instead, and according to our ability attempt to register what happens on the front of our—well, vision, is it not? For there . . . see . . . over there . . . in the narrow trek between the Scylla of Fact and Charybdis of Fiction . . . there is that ambitious passage that, we suspect, corresponds to the proper course an essay should take—and look: there . . . all of a sudden . . . no, there . . . further up . . . yes . . . there is that star, so oddly shaped, almost like an angular bobbin, in fact, that is likely to be our sole guide in this gray pursuit: the terrible, the sweet, the eternal Why (more about this later).

In order to give uncertainty its due, however, perhaps we should begin by sucking our lip for a bit—just to grant ourselves time enough to renegotiate the terms of our toil. No? Wait for second thoughts to drop as coins to the ground, then? Or simply play with the remaining change in our pockets, moving it about while fixing our fazed focus on the twilight territory ahead of us? And in every movement of migratory thought try to decipher something hostile or foreign? Or, if neither, at least unusual ways in which it might appear? Or, on the contrary, rise and straighten up, as stiffly spined as a rake, and read the arabesques of smoke that trail from our cigarette as if they were written in the flowery longhand of true yearning? And thereafter permit alertness to slacken, dreams to distract us, and semi-autonomous notions of relaxation to divert our fingers long enough for them to release their hold on the situation? And then grip again . . . release again . . . and so forth, and so on . . . But: why? Purely to demonstrate that spirited laxity and tender resolve that are needed to persevere in the quaint enterprise of falling asleep with awareness intact. And then declare to ourselves, as Kinbote did to Shade: "You really should promise to use all that wonderful stuff, you bad gray poet, you"? Or straightforwardly confess, as Adam von Librikov once did, that "My belief in the phantomatic nature of my existence entitled me to certain amusements"? And therefore, gray gods willing, allow that "something" to catch our attention that is and is not us, yet always seems gray?

Yes . . . well . . . it might do. But it all seems so *contrived*. And as unavailing as the mirror image of Narcissus slammed flat against the drab underside of the well's surface. Really. Would it not be sufficient to loiter a little, like a backward train of thought, and drowsily dwell on the necessities of, say, definition? There is a decent topic for an essay. No threshold existence without demarcation. In the process, we may seek out some ether revenants to keep us company . . . contours containing nothing but errant air and oblivion . . . and even take stock of a phantom or two . . . yes, certainly some phantoms . . . some apparitions of questionable solidity, that is, and some of memory's spectral antics . . . as well as the humming haze that our ears, curled like question marks, seem to bracket as the shady figure of sleep approaches. In other words: stick to vagueness. In all its states, fashions, and forms: sometimes dull and sluggish, sometimes lithe and risqué, but sometimes also so subtly stirring as to mimic the neat whir of wheels we may make out behind the flat plate of time, running smooth fingers across the neutral face of a clock—for time is what this is about, is it not; i.e., a bout of grayness?

Neither scholarly account nor personal fabrication, then; just an attempt to seize that defiant "something." Let the hand we conjured forth try to hold on to it. There you go. Easy, you know, does it. "An Essay About Nothing," as Fielding termed it. Or: Aspects of a Gray Spell.

OK. As you please. Have it your way. But if the "theme of the book is simple," as *The Real Life of Sebastian Knight* claims— let us say

A man is dying: you feel him sinking throughout the book; his thoughts and memories pervade the whole with greater or lesser distinction (like the swell and fall of uneven breathing), now rolling up this image, now that, letting it ride in the wind, or even tossing it out on the shore, where it seems to move and live for a minute on its own and presently is drawn back again by gray seas where it sinks or is strangely transfigured.

—with what will it be written? Who is the umbral companion that assists our present hand in this silly bounty of dispensations? What, pray, causes fingers created with such amateurish ease to inspire shapes, at a distance, that to eyes less willingly deceived have the whole area of life or of death?

"Not a pencil in the street but has this awful power," Emily Dickinson once wrote in a late poem, having asked the last question we just posed, rather exultantly, as our own, "though nobody arrests it." This "awful power": we shall retain it like the remission now sensed in spine and digits. It may account for Nabokov's transfiguration in "gray seas." (Oh, that sinking feeling.)

Empty-handed we may be at first, but will not so remain. Thus, let us sample, yes, let us sample our first refrain:

> If it had no pencil
> Would it try mine—
> Worn—now—and dull—sweet,
> Writing much to thee.
> If it had no word,
> Would it make the Daisy,
> Most as big as I was,
> When it plucked me?

The "slip of paper" on which these lines once were scattered like the pigeons outside our window was "signed 'Emily,'" according to one editor of her poems, and . . . ah, not to forget . . . "pinned together around the stub of a pencil." So. There. It is. Our first specimen. Not much to look at. Not much of anything, to be frank. Worn and torn and tugged, whittled down rather bluntly, too, and with a coat the color of an old contusion. Shall we nonetheless . . .

well . . . try . . . pluck . . . glean it . . . or first probe some other samples from the art of disappearance the process in which we are bound to remain?

Right then. We shall return to it. Instead? Instead enter desolate Mr. Malone, courtesy of Samuel Beckett. He is in the process of discussing his favorite pastimes when suddenly interrupted. An unexpected patch of white space opens up on the printed page, two days and two nights pass, then Malone resumes again:

> What a misfortune, the pencil must have slipped from my fingers, for I have only just succeeded in recovering it after forty-eight hours . . . of intermittent efforts.

Deploring "the whole sorry business" of being Malone, praising instead "the blessedness of absence," Beckett's pitiable hero continues by describing the tiny tool, not unsimilar to that of Dickinson, which has caused all the trouble:

> My pencil. It is a little Venus, still green no doubt, with five or six facets, pointed at both ends and so short there is just room, between them, for my thumb and the two adjacent fingers, gathered together in a little vice. I use the two points turn and turn about, sucking them frequently, I love to suck. And when they go quite blunt I strip them with my nails which are long, yellow, sharp and brittle for want of chalk or is it phosphate. So little by little my little pencil dwindles, inevitably, and the day is fast approaching when nothing will remain but a fragment too tiny to hold.

A figure of finitude in truth, Malone's pencil, or what remains of it, does not sport the yellow coat favored by most of its compeers, but is a shabby, green little Venus, with a handful of facets and sharpened at both ends. Yet "the strange thing," confesses Malone,

> is I have another pencil, made in France, a long cylinder hardly broached, in the bed with me somewhere I think.

Ah, in bed with a pencil, is it? Some pastime, indeed. Let us grope for that other, precious divertissement among the sheets and pillows, and let us hope it is slim, yellow, and civil the way pencils are supposed to be. There is not much light around to go by, however; it "is the same gray as heretofore," Malone confesses, "literally sparkling at times, then growing murky and dim, thickening is perhaps the word, until all things are blotted out except the window which seems in a manner of speaking to be my umbilicus." So we shall have to rely on our fingers' own sense of purpose.

If the bed will be the main stage of this affair, however, and malfeasance spell its purpose, perhaps we ought to spend a thought or two on our company. "A little vice" may be a temporary thing, but it is not to be taken lightly. So, then, whose company do we seek? And what kind of moment will be the most opportune for its attainment? These are the confessions of Zeno easing into their beginning like our hand presently into the sheets' vast and unknown interior:

> I seem to be able to see my thoughts as something quite apart from myself. I can watch them rising, falling, their only form of activity. I seize my pencil in order to remind them that it is the duty of thought to manifest itself. At once the wrinkles collect on my brow as I think of the letters that make up every word. The present surges up and dominates me, the past is blotted out.

Such, indeed, seems the moment we will speak of . . . speak at . . . no, speak *in*: unruly, uncertain, and changing. As if we were gulping down, between "the letters that make up every word," the elastic bits of a yawn. Rising and falling. Then rising. Falling and rising. Then falling. Falling. The gray sea. And its drabs of deeds.

Thus we are not likely to court the services of the fountain pen, that resilient supporter of eternity (lean, noble, a sheen), since ink must always be supplied and never ceases to flicker or flow. Nor shall we, moving down the ladder of stylic distinction, flirt with its paunchy compeer, the ball-point pen, which spreads its bowls into words as generously as the adulterer his flattery. With its shimmering praise, it, too, tries to eternalize the said. Neither quill, feather, nor plume, then, nor Bic, marker, or rolling ball . . . neither clay, nor chalk, nor crayon . . . no, none of that ever more. For us, fumbling with the tardiness of the hour, there is only the tool with the terrible power.

"Yesterday I tried to let myself go completely," Svevo has Zeno confess:

> The result was that I fell into a deep sleep and experienced nothing except a great sense of refreshment, and the curious sensation of having seen something important while I was asleep. But what it was I could not remember; it had gone forever.
>
> But today this pencil will prevent my going to sleep. I dimly see certain strange images that have no connection with my past; an engine puffing up a steep incline dragging endless coaches. Where can it all come from? Where is it going? How did it get there in the first place?

Yes, only the pencil, thus obliquely inclined, is to be our reprieve from a sleep as profound—to create a rickety rhyme—as that of those who reap the rest that is ceaselessly deep. The gray sea, that, and therefore this: a yellow straw. (Remember Malone's umbilicus?) It is going to end up short, of course, we know that, like words tumbling toward exhaustion across sheets of whitish insurrection dreaming they will not, or—to stay metamorphorical—the drowner's fumbling string of gasps as he is about to give in to a rescue anything but safe. Little to trust, and even less to handle. But however nuggatory and barren, with shavings shed and sheddings shunned, it is still a straw straining to avail the ailing.

Let us locate this thin figure of finitude before the hour gets too tardy and apprehension makes us retract the present advances of our . . . oh, too late, here it comes—the question: But is it, then? Is it the straw of proverbial rescue? Or is it the draw the link the pull the lead instead?

"A straw?," Kafka demanded in one of his octavo books, and added (we should have known):

> Many keep themselves above water with the stroke of a pencil. Keep themselves? Like the drowner, dream of rescue.

There you go.

If, in the following, we will rely on the stroke of a pencil to frame the contours of a vagueness that has already begun to surround us the way dust collects quietly under our bed, it is not to dodge the unavoidable, but merely to drag out the line under which our troubles shall, at length, be summarized. It keeps us going, you may say, like a train toiling toward its distant destination. (We must try to remain in that elastic n-o-w.) Regardless of its situation, of course, such an act of attentive retention will lead to our involuntary sinking into the story of the chosen object—much as when, having treaded on a wobbly spot, we sense something vital giving way, and we sink, suddenly and vertically, in a newborn element, unlike anything previously known, through several strata of shimmering wilderness and gray, velvety delight, until we come to trust this descending repose as if it contained the solution to that most nightmarish of impossibilities: to swindle death. But then, as there can be no release from destiny, we will have to come to terms with this, too. At least we shall remember to call for some ease as long as we can. Mnemosyne, then. Although she can be, at times, a careless girl, or so it has been claimed, we will prevail by proceeding in her penumbral tow. For "memory," too, is "a straw," Walter Benjamin reminds us, and while its images, as well as their after-images, those retinal revenants roaming through recollection, do not need to bear much resemblance to any personal past, and no real relation to it as far as we can tell, we had better latch on to their shadowy succession. Hook,
li n
        e,
              a
                      n
                          d
                                  si
                                      n
                                        k
                                          e
                                            r.

As it were.

Like the dull succession of nights and days that has been our listless lot, the end of that slack stroke is clear from the beginning, but the beginning itself remains shrouded in distance and unknowing. From where did it come? How did it get there? And, well, why?

Hearsay has it, or legend has it, or better still, the notion is afloat, that the trail, sign, queue left by our chosen object may be tracked back to an oak, or possibly an ash, on a slope in northern England. During a stormy night the tree is said to have fallen and where earlier its roots had rested, branching out in secret security, now gleamed the gray promise of a different order (hence future). This happened in Borrowdale in the Lake District, the year was the Lord's fifteen-hundred-and-sixty-fifth, and on the throne was Elizabeth. So much for where for now. As to the how, well, a wandering hunter, "attracted by the particles of a strange, black substance clinging to the roots of the fallen tree," called the unexpected discovery to the attention of the locals, and shortly thereafter excavations commenced. Wadd had been found; now it began to be fostered and fiddled; later it would be defended.

Still, the where and the how are somewhat fuzzy in contour, like furniture in the dark, and the origins of the mystery uncovered remain wrapped in the hissing softness of obscurity. Thus, for example, writes one chronicler about the region:

> The recorded history of wadd is patchy and largely unreliable, as is the case, too, with Keswick's famous pencil industry. Seatoller Fell [where the ancient wadd holes are], both literally and figuratively, is mist-distorted: distant rocks, looming through the fog like Peruvian pinnacles, dwindle, when approached, into stones a few feet high; Greenland bears some sheep; wadd, an established commercial commodity for over 300 years, proves amazingly elusive. The quest for its story . . . developed for the author into an almost Alice-like adventure; the nearer she drew to wadd, the further did wadd recede.

As if this were not enough, Molly Lefebure points out that the pencil's elusiveness may also be discerned in the bountiful explanations proffered concerning its alleged origin:

Reading up wadd one discovers that most of the authorities are merely repeating the words of a previous writer; thus one digs one's way downwards through a slag-heap of endless (and sometimes erroneous) repetition.

The wadd, according to legend, was discovered originally by shepherds, after a large ash-tree on the fellside (an alternative version of the tale gives it as an oak) had been uprooted by a gale. The date of the discovery is unknown. When first found the substance was simply used by the local people for marking their sheep (continues the legend).

Continues the legend, we could continue, if we want to widen the hole of discovery to allow other tales, tall as well as thin, to fit in, or mark the cattle perceived through Lefebure's account with signs as erratic as question marks (an allusion whose shadowy fleece we promise shall later be shorn). For the moment, however, suffice it to observe that if our object's beginning is uprooted, lacking as it does the where's withhall and about, its attribution is likely to be as legendary as any other account creduously contrived.

Let us maintain a measure of probity, therefore, as we poke our way through the sheets, and enlist evidence in support of an inkling already prepared to turn conjecture. The first item to be displayed begins by ending, as it properly should, and proceeds from the chambers of Nabokov, an eminence a color in no need of mention. In *Invitation to a Beheading*, he recalls Cincinnatus C., who, sentenced to death, "dreamed that he walked on water" and has only one chance of surviving himself:

> On the table glistened a clean sheet of paper and, distinctly outlined against this whiteness, lay a beautifully sharpened pencil, as long as the life of any man except Cincinnatus, and with an ebony gleam to each of its six facets. An enlightened descendant of the index finger. Cincinnatus wrote: "In spite of everything I am comparatively. After all I had premonitions, had premonitions of this finale."

True, this is a gauche way to begin a book, but if we follow the clue Nabokov trusts us to pick up—like the lead in lead that did not go unnoticed—we find already in this backhanded sort of opening the resolution to the ending that is his book's beginning. Cincinnatus is not only a name, but also an intimation (as discreet as an eyebrow raised by a Latin lover) of ornamental language or flowery style, and thus might be considered a figure for literature. (Let us call it, simply, a sample of *fioriture*.) So much for the vagaries of dim wheres and leaden hows. Thanks to the freedom granted by their ambiguity, Nabokov is able carefully to expand a vanishing moment to encompass an entire life. (And he does it, finally, in a manner that must be the dream of every writer: by making the work's interior contain its exterior. (Strange, strange world.)) If we prefer to call our hero C., then, it is not to be less ornamental, but simply to stress his existence's elastic brevity. Turned around and given a twitch as artful as the knots on Nabokov's plot line, such abbreviation might also fit into the tight drape of a mark conniving to become question, which would in fact better suit his ornate prose . . . like a coiling snake its cryptic skin. (Figure that.)

When we first meet C., he is sitting in his prison cell "with its peephole like a leak in a boat," and we quickly approach the ending although we have read pages fewer even than the fingers with which we hold our book:

> The right-hand, still untasted part of the novel, which, during our delectable reading, we would lightly feel, mechanically testing whether there were still plenty left (and our fingers were always gladdened by the placid, faithful thickness) has suddenly, for no reason at all, become quite meager: a few minutes of quick reading, already downhill, and—O horrible!

The ending, thus, is clear from the beginning—it is all downhill from here—we know—though the beginning proper has found no explanation. But *Invitation to a Beheading* is a moment of death, drastically speaking, bracketed like hands cupping the fragile flame of a candle, and on good grounds we may surmise that it must remain less important to determine when it began than to postpone its inescapable extinction—such, at any rate, is "the dramatic privilege of drowning individuals," according to *Pnin* ("especially in the former Russian Navy"). In short and sum, thus: it is not surprising that the brevity of C.'s life provokes him—as it did Malone—to take up writing, despite its being a cliché as worn as the springs in his cell bed. Only by framing candle into flicker, then its lucent fuss into a candid story, will he know he is not yet defunct. While C. does not know his exact mortal hour, his pencil has lost "more than a third of its length" already, so we should not be surprised if he insists on a certain kind of slowness, no, on a much needed "discretion":

> In my case discretion requires that I think in terms of very small numbers—but that is all right, that is all right—I am alive. I had a strange sensation last night—and it was not the first time—: I am taking off layer after layer, until at last . . . I do not know how to describe it, but I know this: through the process of gradual divestment I reach the final, indivisable, firm, radiant point, and this point says: I am! like a pearl ring embedded in a shark's gory fat—O my eternal, my eternal.

Progressively smaller . . . gradually diminishing . . . slowly but unavoidably stripped of cover and robbed of bulk . . . yes . . . yes . . . yet abiding, abiding. O. That speck of self in nothingness. A leaden little vestige, a point of void. Still, however miniscule, it is enough; "actually nothing more is necessary." While C. merely delays what will come—and is, therefore, "comparatively"—his desire to express himself thus manages to extend fact into fiction, deed into diction, and hence diminutive existence into roundabout being.

Yet, of course, as a figure, however gray, he *is* not in proper terms, but only "through an error—not in this prison, specifically—but in this whole terrible, striped world" (all straws are calamitous, we take it, one way or the other).

> And now I am losing some thread, which I held so palpable only a moment ago. Where is it? It has slipped out of my grasp! I am trembling over the paper, chewing the pencil through the lead, hunching over to conceal myself from the door through which a piercing eye stings me in the nape.

> Panic, terror . . . madness . . . error . . . white, nightmarish loss . . . Smell the air of bliss and oblivion descending on the scene with

that hot hum of mendacity, like a swiftly kindling, swindling cloud. Disapperance seems but another name for fate. For, of course, whatever the place, and whatever the concern—indeed, whatever the point of comparison (there will be more than one for us to turn to)—C. remains a prisoner in the handsome cell between our distant fingers whose door chink we may choose to close at any instant. His straw of rescue is but a skid of pencil, after all, easily torn, easily revoked, ever so easily erased. Thus, such too, must be the skittish stroke we shall try to follow—down, then down again, it will go: a means to the end that is beginning. That will be our point of departure, at any rate—and this will be our point of return: a dim dot suspended within a cupped frame gradually contracting into an involute abode, delighted to play a part in assuming the form of $x, y \ldots z \ldots$ and then: nevermore.

The next piece of evidence we wish to present, though not as circumloquaciously, also belongs within the precincts of Nabokov's prose. In *Transparent Things*, he continues to demonstrate the strange power that C. discovered is inherent in writing with a pencil. In the novel's opening, Hugh Person, its main character and no less duplicitous a figure than his *semblable*, his *frère*, is studying something he has found forgotten in a desk drawer in a hotel room to which he returns like the shadow of a former self:

> The pencil has been worn down to two-thirds of its original length. The bare wood of its tapered end has darkened to plumbeous plum, thus merging in tint with the blunt tip of graphite whose blind gloss alone distinguishes it from the wood. A knife and a brass sharpener have thoroughly worked upon it and if it were necessary we could trace the worked upon fate of the shavings, each mauve on one side and tan on the other when fresh, but now reduced to atoms of dust whose wide, wide dispersal is panic catching its breath. . . . On the whole, it whittled sweetly, being of an old-fashioned make. Going back a number of seasons (not as far, though, as Shakespeare's birth year when pencil lead was discovered) and then picking up the thing's story again in the "now" direction, we see graphite, ground very fine, being mixed with moist clay by young girls and old men. This mass, this pressed caviar, is placed in a metal cylinder which has a blue eye, a sapphire with a hole drilled in it, and through this the caviar is

forced. It issues in one continuous appetizing rodlet . . . , which looks as if it retained the shape of an earthworm's digestive tract . . . It is now being cut into the lengths required for these particular pencils (we glimpse the cutter, old Elias Borrowdale, and are about to mouse up his forearm on a side trip of inspection but we stop, stop and recoil, in our haste to identify the individual segment). See it baked, see it boiled in fat (here a shot of the butcher, a shot of the shepherd, a shot of the shepherd's father, a Mexican) and fitted into the wood.

Now let us not lose our precious bit of lead while we prepare the wood. Here's the tree! *This* particular pine! It is cut down. Only the trunk is used, stripped of its bark. We hear the whine of a newly invented power saw, we see logs being dried and planed. Here's the board that will yield the integument of the pencil in the shallow drawer (still not closed). We recognize its presence in the log as we recognized the log in the tree and the tree in the forest and the forest in the world that Jack built. We recognize that presence by something that is perfectly clear to us but nameless, and as impossible to describe as a smile to somebody who has never seen smiling eyes.

Thus the entire little drama, from crystallized carbon and felled pine to this humble implement, to this transparent thing, unfolds in a twinkle.

Behind each image others contrive to reside . . . this drilled hole, that pressed caviar . . . Borrowdale . . . our precious bit of lead . . . wide wide dispersal . . . and every now contains other nows like train schedules in countries less punctilious than Hugh's adopted land of the Alps.

Two pieces of evidence, then, of fabulous procreation. We need no more. They will suffice. They will do. Let us move instead to "the terrible, eternal why" of which Baudelaire spoke, which is really The Question of Vagueness As Met in Literature, and eye the letters that Zeno asserted "make up every word." They will become our main affair and only company, and thus deserve scrutiny no less embellished than the attention C. pays to his two thirds of a pencil. But better proceed leisurely, calmly, with that trotting sway familiar to sheep. "Sinking slowly inside a syllable," remarks a critic whose subclauses sit as securely as the Colt in the shepherd's holster, we shall then "discover distinct connections of another kind":

An object taken from a drawer, as a pencil is shuddered from its rest in an old desk, has not been held there by wood and physics through the years, nor does it appear now in obedience to our hero's rough tug, as some wordly pencil might. It comes to light because it has a place in the Divine Plan, otherwise a dead moth might have slid to view instead . . . a matchbook, bridge tally, or a medal. Once we make that move which Nabokov, in *Transparent Things*, so movingly describes, and pass into the state of being of his books, forgotten pencils, mislaid memories, discarded persons, all the meaningless moments that make up life (each day nothing but a noisy rain of accidents like a spill of beans) are transformed, for now every item is a passage . . . is a peephole where eyes can be seen staring at staring eyes.

In the scene already cited, and now recited, Nabokov describes the predicaments of the tool he uses as he draws the life story of a pencil—all unfolding in a twinkle, ever expandable, in the manner of a very dry eye. A moving movement, it is. (And promiscuous, too, as we shall see in the pages to ensue: not more than a conjunction and preposition . . . as well as a correlative construction . . . compressed into that handy diminutive *as* . . . as thin as the hardworking air extending itself through the drowner's trough of a throat . . . *as this, as that . . . as if . . . as . . . as* . . . but in the course unfolding—through that "process of gradual divestment" of which C. spoke—it may yield our Why as the old *eallswa* once gave way to, well, a swell . . . dental, hissing, monosyllabic . . . yet tied to time and figure-producing, it stretches the fabric of the spoken moment, allowing it to contain simultaneity as well as similitude.)

For our purposes most pressing and present, moving at more than one remove now from Nabokov's transformations, we best squint a mite—and our object will look like the straw the sight of which we should not like to lose. Not too soon, at any rate; not now, no, not yet. Twinkling light, it is, and yellow at that. Whatever its origin—slope, drawer, or magician's pocket—it amounts to the same whether it sheds itself on the beginning we just saw contrived or becomes one in retrospect, since the perception occasioned by this light (and with what lawless lucidity) offers a beginning though things may not begin there, in the same way that

Hugh Person's pencil provides an opening although it does not begin in the flat-bottomed middle drawer of the old desk, "relegated to a dark corner of the room" in which he is trying to install himself (recalling, rather, a vanishing point—reminiscent of the manner in which one bracketed clause may disappear inside another—or some other marker of flat inner infinity) . . . and eyes are seen staring at staring eyes . . . not for the last time, nor for the first.

Let this yellow emergence be our essay's signal for getting underway, like the sign once indicated to Rilke's dishevelled Malte:

> How came that little gray woman to stand once for a whole quarter of an hour by my side in front of a shop window, showing me an old, long pencil, that was thrust with infinite slowness from her villainous, clenched hands? I pretended to look at the articles displayed in the window and not to notice anything. But she knew that I had seen her, she knew that I stood there wondering what she was really doing. For I understood quite well that the pencil in itself was of no consequence; I felt that it was a sign, a sign for the initiated, a sign that the outcasts know. I guessed she was indicating to me that I should go somewhere or do something. And the strangest thing about the whole affair was that I could not rid myself of the feeling that there actually existed a certain compact to which this sign belonged, and that this scene was in truth something that I should have expected.

An indication, then, and not what it points to. A clue has been given, and although we do not know what it is or what it may mean, why, why, why (the whys of happenstance as so many x's), or for that matter whether we should be "in" the know, the now that we know we are in expands like a gray area with limits not yet visible. So this will be our realm. Between sign and significance. Or gesture and gist. Made of a vagueness lazily lasting like mist. Being without being; a bracketful of "it"—"(still not closed)," to reiterate Hugh Person's formula. But as long as we stay within—in bed, truth to tell—we will be as safe as in the swelling sway of the sea. Notwithstanding. Nonetheless. Now.

Only the matter, then, remains of deciding how to devise an account of this interlude, a shrubbery in grayish bloom. Thus far, we concede, it has taken shape rather haphazardly, like scrambled eggs, so we would do well to give it another firmness, if we may, and a trajectory with as much verve, curve, and span as we can master, no muster. Perhaps a second hand is what is needed to keep us afloat. . . . Or. Well. No. Let us not think too much (it is bound to get us into trouble), but simply concoct another hand, quickly, and then count its members, assigning to the sturdiest the task of indicating our bearing—thus also to stand for this slope of an introduction so negatively inclined—and to the remaining of revealing one, two . . . three . . . four different versions of the vagueness found in literature. Then we will have a full hand for our essay. In none of the cases, however, shall we consider tradition more than necessary, and we will always skirt unity and opt for the plain. There will be no elements of classical disposition, we can promise, nor any mention of temperaments, bodily fluids, or their astral alikes (with one exception, perhaps: thinly-loined melancholy). Our first version, rather, will vie with water and be its selfmade same, that is, it will investigate that wailing discharge that amounts to tears ample and plain . . . the second will avoid fire crackling and its curly flame, and instead seek its fume, smoke, and vapor, trailing in vain, while the third will collect dirt and dust, rather than earth and its drain, and thus be reckoned, well, be reckoned then as grain . . . and the last . . . concerning the last of our elements thus sustained, we shall in air seek what is nebulous in name but credulous just the same—appearing as clouds, that is, neither as fog nor as rain.

And this will be our order of procedure. First we shall call on Pinkie to signal thrill and action—something may be needed, after all, to entice us to continue (a shade of pale violence, perhaps, like that tinge they term gridelin); then we would like to skip convention for a moment extended like, well, a hand, and engage the longest of our friends—Finger for short—since our second concern will conclude by adding to our initial taint of commotion some ruffles of bodily pleasure we shall clothe in grenat hues; on our third count we shall make up for the lapse thus created by backtracking a bit and settle for the digit with the ring in order to signal renewed commitment to our task; while last, and forth, we shall raise the index, saved until now, as it will remind us of the danger looming increasingly dark and dull, whose *pointe assassine* our hand thus cupped and equipped will try, but fail, to stall from coming.

If this solution seems to avoid nuance and complication, we would do well to express regret, of course, hands down, but also to remember that the angular figure of four, as immovable as a pillow of rubber, still offers us access to every cranny, corner, nook, and thimble into which we should like to poke. Simplicity is not perforce simplification, and sumptuous reduction will remain the one rule we will not be likely to break, as safe as the minus sign that is the horizon for each and all of us. And is it necessary to add that the one principle we will finally come to embrace, settling then for that rubber, is The Iron Law of Gray: an indifference that makes a difference?

This, at any rate, seems to be what the nameless mouth tells us in the third part of Beckett's trilogy, proposing that it is simply

> gray we need, to begin with, because of what it is, and of what it can do, made of bright and black, able to shed the former, or the latter, and be the latter or the former alone.

To begin, then, we shall need only this gray gorge, we who are in the gray, inclined to harbor gray thoughts, but also victims, in the gray, of gray itself, whatever it might be and whatever it might do . . . surrounded by the unhurried smoke wafting through this sullen February day, sitting in a solitary room where the floor trembles, but only a little, almost imperceptibly, because a bell struck seven or eight and the reverberations spread like rumors through a prison, yet as they increase it feels as if an air conditioner has started its labors in the apartment below, or maybe it is an old refrigerator, and it suddenly seems, in fact, as if we were out on the gray sea that expands in front of our window on the second floor, on a bark or a ship with no rudder, perhaps, moving heaving hauling itself forward thanks to an underground of bellows, pipes, pistons, hydraulic pumps, hoppers, and tubes (a belly-shaped Hades floating on a water with neither banks nor beaches), but that seems to have developed trouble, puff, and run

into difficultieesss-h. In our dreams we are often down there, in these undermost regions, and then it is as if we are no longer at home, but in a cool spacious expanse—cell clause sanctum—and from a window on the first floor could see a bare blackish-gray fire wall spreading out in four different directions but only two cardinal points, brick upon brick upon brick, as if ten times ten thousand identical squares could be a paraphrase of freedom. Dreams are nomadic like that and may wander, if they wish, as memories from one to another (what I recall is never what you remember, but your memory is still mine), stone upon stone upon stone creating that mnemonic castle, yet despite the monotony of these ten times ten thousand reiterations, their combinations are both boundless and inexhaustible. They can always build new walls; form other existences; harbor unknown experiences. Next to the fire wall, for example, we notice a staircase well winding itself like a tower being sharpened down, though we cannot see the blunt spiral from where we are sitting placed in front of different squares and another form of freedom. Yet we begin to recognize ourselves, of course, dimly, with the hazy reluctance of surface sleepers, and most probably we would be correct in believing that we are in fact in our own backyard and in the skullscape of . . . well, whom? A drizzle of daylight leans over the edge, slips on the
newly tarred roof, and, beginning to roll down in abundant
beams, fuzzy and inexplicable, it is sharpened to points
of gleaming darkness as it falls in chips, chunks, and
flakes—a wide wide world of dispersal—falling,
plunging, tumbling—but also winding itself—and really only winding itself—
down into that gray gorge of a backyard, like a drilling auger or the
mirror image of a tower,
an incidental wedge or
some hardened
little point

. .
.

a bottomless gulf that is a mouth and an opening after all, a void-voice and nothing else in fact, a wounded wary weeping embouchement that spits and sputters and sobs and gargles and curses, but quietly also dreams of softening the pointed lead with its dull luster, held in our unstable hand.

For . . . yes . . . we did find it, and we have picked it up.

So this is what it has come to, this is what it will be. A now threadbare and thin. Let us try to remain in it, though, as we are sinking downward inside its elastic pocket of textured nonexistence. Perhaps our movement will stir some scraps of memory into life . . . or at least a limber splinter of imagery or two . . . and if not, the lunulae to our sides, embracing us in their taut and thrumming way (really, without being, they support our being), will help us . . . concocting dim figurations of thought like those bits of phantomatic plastic that, rustling in a gray kaleidoscope, offer shapes and patterns of sensuous nullity. The trail we shall follow will dwindle, of course, we know that, first it will begin to fade, slowly eking out of sight, then it will recede more seriously, until it simply will vanish like a sinker into another, deeper depth, but such is the lead in any lead. Not to be argued with. (Just as little as with the cut of an umbilical chord.)

Now, then. Let us clasp our fingers tighter around that lean, yellow straw and begin this essay before it is too late. A little vice, yes? So be it. Wood will have to be scraped, lead squandered, and the rest is the risky business of fingers four and fumbling. Now. Let us begin. Yes, let us begin now. Again and again again.

§ One

Like charcoal-colored magnets to a humming refrigerator door, advocates of pedagogy stick to the opinion that the force of example is greater than that of law. And there is pull to such truth, of course, since to argue that the rule and not the accident create the thief would be almost criminal. Let us close in on a few samples, then, without much further ado, stalking the coolly rumbling machine like the private eye a potential suspect, and clip them with what will serve as our only—but then our very own—magnet catch: "gray literature."

Assigned a precise if contested definition, tucked away in language's obscurity like an old garment in the back of a closet, gray literature properly speaking is neither a contrivance as convenient but insubstantial as a McGuffin, nor a fated fabrication created for us by muddled *fiat*. On the contrary, according to C. P. Auger's *Information Sources in Gray Literature*, the term classifies publications "not readily available through normal bookselling channels, and therefore difficult to identify and obtain." Such materials include reports, records, and specifications of technical nature, but also summations of conferences and offprints of all kinds, translations, government publications, and supplementary data, as well as texts dealing in commerce and marketing. Sharing a number of characteristics with what we believe to perceive in our chosen color, this literature is distinguished by being available through restricted access, which may provide us with one instructive indication, to which can be added not only qualities such as poor bibliographic control, unprofessional layout, and limited editions (shady literature, in short), but also an attribute more essential for our present purposes: its informal, even unconventional character.

Although it might cause concern among librarians, those gray guardians of print, we would like to pull the designation out of its umbral den, brushing off age, oddity, and seclusion, and let it stand for the wayward way of writing for which alone we will try to polish attention and force our focus. Auger even speaks of an "indicator of uncertainty, vagueness, and imprecision." Honoring the memory of Rilke's shabby lady in front of a Parisian shop window, we would like to propose this pointer or extended index—this the most unstable of straws—as our particular guide to gray literature. D. G. van der Heij, whose anonymous initials, as in the case of Auger, point to a different order of twilight (which we regret to have to leave in the dark, like a shadow reported missing), even describes such literature as "fugitive" and "invisible." And to this evasive writing belongs a vagueness that is as fundamental as cuffs and pomade to earlier generations, whose local appearances we propose to term, simply, "gray areas."

So then, this will be the affair of our tool, the purpose of our toil: to investigate a handful of areas of gray literature in which evanescence alone may be counted on. To the best of our abilities we shall try to trace them like that lively thread that is likely to be our only lead. We find a first sample at the source, or at least at the source of one tradition, and it will indicate to us on which water to write. For whether mutinous and violent, like a hose uncoiled and stiffening, or silent, vast, and dark, like some intergalactic lake in a burnt-out solar system, water constitutes time taking form, and thus provides us with our Prima Materia . . . First Factor . . . Inaugural Element . . . By this mutable matter—blue as ink and its hovering hue—writhingly white as a beam of lather—jet black as the finest satin of nightfall—we also recover an initial case of the liquid transience known as tears, our personal preference among the element's forms of apparition.

"Achilles went away," it is stated some three-hundred-and-fifty lines into the first book of *The Iliad* (and already we find reason to suspect that we shall never move toward a gray zone, but only away from the familiar in order to possibly reach it; gray appears to be the color of withdrawal, an art of departure). The hero "sat apart from his companions," Homer informs us,

> at the gray sea,
> weepingly looking out on infinite water.

Here is our first place, our original topos. Raise the pinkie and remember: everything begins on a beach, by the sedated sea, confronting infinity. And it begins, as we shall see, by ending. In tears.

Separated from his peers, Achilles has seated himself "out of sight," untouchable like the eight ball in a game of pool. The hero of the first Homeric epic is sad and somber, cut down by despondency. Agamemnon, king of Argos and commander-in-chief of the consolidated Greek army, has just insulted the Myrmidon by taking for himself the gift Achilles had received in the war against the Trojans, "the beautifully girdled" Briseis. The humiliation began when Calchas, the seer, predicted that the anger that the Greeks were attracting from "the god who strikes from a distance"—far-shooting Apollo—had its cause in the offense suffered by the priest Chryses: abducted like a whiff of prized incense, his daughter had been given to Agamemnon as fair war booty. Apollo, it is made clear, will not

> drive this shameful destruction from the Argives,
> not till we give back the girl with sparkling eyes
> to her loving father—no price, no ransom paid—
> and carry a sacred hundred bulls to Chryses's town.

Enraged by the prophesy, scorched like dry wood, the Argives' hot-headed king refuses to understand why he shall lose his gift rather than one of the other generals—powerful Ajax from Salamis, the tall Cretan Idomeneus, Laertes's crafty son Odysseus, or the greatest man of all in war, the Pelide Achilles. But there is little to say, and even less to do, against a fate carrying the imprimatur of gods.

After deliberations and appeals, better suitable to a playground than a war council, Odysseus returns Chryseis to her father, the prescribed hecatomb is sacrificed, and as a result Apollo is appeased, no longer "scourging Argos's army with dreadful plagues."

Appropriate amends made, the problem ought to vanish like tired ghosts in the shy hours of morning, thus allowing the ten-year old war to reach an un-tragical ending, at least as seen from the standpoint of the Greeks, and especially its Myrmidonian contingent. But Agamemnon will not agree to remain without loot: after row and rumpus, he demands to be awarded the booty already given to Achilles. The leader of the Myrmidons "may be exceedingly god-like and excellent," but why should he remain empty-handed who wields command over the entire Greek army, including the Pelide himself?

It is the epilogue to this request we are witnessing as Achilles sits down by that leaden ocean. But we also read the fragment of a quotation, sticking to the narrative like a piece of adhesive tape. Already two hundred lines earlier, before the epic barely had found time to usher its readers into its interior, Chryses did something similar when he implored the Greeks to release his daughter against a royal ransom. Unlike the other Acheans, Agamemnon was scandalized by the request and chased the priest away with words compacted and hurled at him like stones. "The old man was terrified. He obeyed the order," we are told,

> turning, trailing away in silence down the shore
> where the roaring battle lines of breakers crash and drag.

Just as Chryses invoked Apollo, imploring the god to assist him against hot-tempered Agamemnon—"Pay the Danaans back—your arrows for my tears!"—that is: send the plague against them—lacrimose Achilles asks his mother Thetis, goddess of the ocean, for help against Argos's haughty king. May the Greeks suffer great losses, so they learn how much they need their fearless warlord in the struggle. This is the prelude to the tale of woe and wail that will make the *Iliad* breathe so heavily, constituting the hub around which its wheel of misfortune shall turn. Achilles, slated the fate of "a life shorter than others," must reestablish his honor, even if the price is unprecedented losses on the Greek side and in addition will cost him his own life.

In order to help wash out the stain on her son's reputation, Thetis appeals to almighty Zeus:

> Come, grant the Trojans victory after victory
> til the Achean armies pay my dear son back,
> building higher the honor he deserves!

At first the Sky-shaker does not answer, but after a while he concedes with sighs as deep as cellars, well aware of what his compliance will bring about. Although both Hera and Pallas Athena, mother and daughter, are rallied against the Trojans and thus oppose him, Zeus promises to "see to this," bringing "it all to pass." The fortune of war turned away from the Acheans, the Trojans, led by mighty Hector, are able to drive the Greeks back all the way to their bellied ships cluttering the beach like so much abandoned attire.

Urged by thwarted generals, Agamemnon sends for Achilles—we are already in the ninth book—but the hero violently resists every attempt to make him rejoin the struggle. His is a body of water no longer connected to the main flow of epic action. It will take another nine books, until the eighteenth, when the Myrmidon's closest friend Patrocles falls clad in his own armor, before Achilles is reconciled with Agamemnon. Only then does he join the struggle's tumult again, a flooding force of nature, taking revenge for Patrocles by slaying in turn his slayer, Hector. The Trojans' fate thus sealed, they know that after their leader's demise, brutal as only a *force majeure* can be, their city is heading for certain downfall. The bullwark protecting them has given way; the course of destiny, the tide of defeat, is upon them. But Achilles's own fate, too, is sealed through this death, as it is stated that the angered Pelide shall succumb not long after the best warrior among the Trojans has fallen. "With tears streaming," Thetis states before Achilles enters the struggle again: "Immediately after Hector's death, fate has prepared your lot."

None of this has happened, however, when we for the first time meet the best of the Acheans alone on the beach, weeping by the ocean. He has not yet spoken to his mother, not yet complained about Agamemnon, and not yet made the decision to withdraw from the raw heat of struggle. Brooding is all. Although the prey, we may guess, of foaming feelings and violent thoughts, certainly gridelin in hue, the Pelide is no longer in action. Despite the affront suffered, however, he has not yet pronounced his retirement from war duty. We catch him at an interim moment, lulling and dull, a pause of dead calm as the sail of epic action is slackened. The ocean, which elsewhere in Homer may froth red like boiling blood or surge heavenly blue like the lined inside of avian wings, now rests immobile as the womb water of still birth. Quiet, silent, indefinable: a gray ocean.

As in the case of Chryses earlier, here, too, there is a crisis of confidence. Set in relief by Achilles's distance from the other Greeks and highlighted by its unusual description, the "gray" ocean is nature's own imprint of the hero's mood. Not only is he dark in mind, but, we must assume, also pale in mien, left speechless by the dishonor inflicted upon him. Homer's projection of Achilles's inner condition, we may thus stop and notice, purposely lacks nimbus and nuance, shades as well as tinges—like the 'shallow water' along the coast implied by the Greek word he uses (*alos*). It is a *blanche mer*, as Mazon's French translation has it, which, if we may continue psychologizing for another dozen or so words, must be as close as we get to the expressionless *in natura*.

If this gray sea corresponds to Achilles's mood, like an ache to its wound, what can be said about the Pelide at this moment is merely that he remains inscrutable—unfathomable as the listless depth under the surging tide and undoubtedly as unfathomable as the pale sky with its loitering clouds. But in both of these images the impenetrable blankness can be ascertained, either thanks to the tide's misty spray or because of the slow drift of indolent vapors. Stated more succinctly: it is *marked*, since without swelling foam or steamy formations there would be nothing to see, only surface or depth, depth or surface, unclear which, but quite certainly something without gradation, nuance, and proportion—much in the way a wad of cotton disintegrated in water is neither wrap nor wrapped, but both. Flat infinity. Endlessly gray. Only a silver coin thrown overboard or a similarly fast falling rain would provide a firmer idea of form, outline, and volume, that trinity of physical philosophy, yet such indications are possible to distill only from Aristotle's *Meteorologica* and similarily climed writings.

Shortly after Homer has moved our minds to spot his hero down by the sea, a load of desolation slumming like a heap of abandoned garment, Achilles throws off the gloom that had descended upon him, turns toward the ocean, and calls on his mother—who hears her son's complaint as she sits on her watery throne, rising from the depth to console him. Taking his hand in hers, Thetis asks him:

> My child—
> why in tears? What sorrow has touched your heart?
> Tell me, please. Do not harbor it deep inside you.
> We must share it all.

But at the moment when our hero is still sitting impassively on the beach, quietly cast yet accurately marked—the shadow of a *Leitmotif*, really—his thoughts are as inscrutable as the eyes of a newborn. And it is this moment, after Homer has disentangled Achilles from the rest of the community but before he has had him call upon his mother for help (this spell of seclusion, this epoch of solitude), which warrants our reflection. For it marks the first identification of individuality in a work that may be characterized by the importance of the personal trait, but surely moves with the collective traffic of myth.

As such it is of particular significance since it dresses its individuation in tender coats of gray. Singularity is here marked not by pomp, circumstance, and typicality, but by an absence of distinction, lack of uniqueness, dearth of detail. It is as if the epic's saturated web of particulars encapsulated a thin but resilient weft that itself displays an almost complete want of what normally makes a thread, red or not, part of a narrative. The scene functions as a knot that arrests attention but also understanding, the importance of which becomes clear only later, yet dully lingers in our mind like the unremarkable interval between the metronome's executions of time. For such is the temporality that defines our hero's situation; a bland period between markings, stresses, or beats, as easily skipped as an exit on a highway, it lacks both Before and After. It would not be telling the entire truth to call it an "interval," then, since such time is created only through repetition. Better would be to say it is a singular phenomenon that nonetheless appears only in plural. Like rain or hair. It is the gray area covered by the eyelid's quick polish of the retina . . . the swift swish of wipers across a windscreen . . . or the blurring oblivion between *tick* and *tack* . . . that beckoning dusk, always unremarkable, behind the dim bars of time. In this gray cell, Achilles sits a prisoner.

As Hans Arp knew, such an epoch of solitude can be coated in only one color:

> I feel how the gray time draws through me.
> It hollows me out.
> It bleaches my dreams.
> For a long time it has been drawing back through me.
> I am lying on the beach by an ocean in ebb
> Next to a fabulous shell.
> It roars and rumbles around me
> And disappears in the depth.
> Slowly the space collapses.
> I am lying on the beach by an ocean in ebb
> Next to a fabulous shell.
> A moon is shining inside.
> A large eye
> A large pearl
> A large tear shine inside.
> I feel how the gray time draws through me.
> For a long time it has been drawing back through me.
> It hollows me out.
> It bleaches my dreams.
> I shake and tremble.

> I crumble.
> My dreams stand like abandoned withered buildings
> On the beach by an ocean in ebb
> Next to a fabulous shell.
> The moons the eyes the pearls the tears crumble.
> I feel how the gray time draws through me.
> For a long time I have been dreaming back.
> I dream myself gray down in the gray depth.

Thus is the time in which Achilles perseveres; without demarcations toward either before or after, cause or effect, as long as he is within it, it merely continues to crumble and corrode. A now without duration, yet never anything else but now. So, then, a bracket, most properly, containing nothingness and desolation, a dim enclosure or a cage of vaporous indistinction . . . a time yard . . . or a lunulous parenthesis . . . reminiscent of lips closed tight and tense, sealing that void that is we when we-less. This liminal zone effaces individuality at the same time as it foregrounds Achilles's singular position in the epic, providing the hero with particularity by robbing him, at the same time, of the active features that alone may corroborate any claims to apartness in a world such as the one captured by Homer.

Yet Achilles's solitude is not entirely passive, because something does indeed happen in the static scene—all stirrings stilled—down by the beach; something is, after all, affirmed. "I am dreaming myself down into the gray depth," the Pelide might have said. His solitude provides a gray moment in a gray area, that much is true, like one among many chalk marks on the prisoner's wall, but it is a nebulous place so filled with uncertainty that it can seek expression only in a language untranslatable into verbal parlance—a language that constitutes a passive activity; what is affirmed, we would like it to be recalled, is tears.

In the same way our tossed silver coin glitters like a herring shoal of one as it recedes deeper into the depth, until it finally disappears with a flash immediately turning up its coat collar, the only remaining trace being the dizzying surface of the water, and in the same way as the falling rain seems to be unscrewed from heavenly tubes to fall toward us from precise points above, until it too blinds us, but this time because our eyes are not able to see clearly because of the tightly sheeted downpour, in much the same manner Achilles's tears mark the result of something to the deeper reason of which we do not have access. They provide clarity without clarification.

Unless affected, tears are normally the effect of something; they have history. Lacrimal emissions, they are the eruption of the Past in the Now. As the result of a previous process, however dry, dark, and remote, Achilles' tears thus encourage us either to seek for a cause or to eke out some allusion to a future effect that might explain aim and intent. *The Iliad*, however, does not provide any clarification for them, be it as a mirror turned toward the past or an arrow directed into the future. Neither properly cause, nor entirely effect, the hero's tears remain inaccessible not only because Homer does not shed light on his solitude—as willy-nilly we do now—but also because the area within which understanding might be sought and secured, like a precious pebble among ordinary gravel, constitutes a gray zone where everything loses contour and distinction. The scene we have happened upon is, rather, an interruption or a caesura, that infinitely small rupture that keeps cause and effect apart. A microchasm. Whoever enters this area, thin as a threshold and as lasting as a ring on water, must relinquish certitude. To begin with.

Silent and remote, Achilles has placed himself outside the circle of friends and realm of action. Inaccessible. It is for this reason—and none other—that his tears provoke the classical question "why?" (Thetis: "My child, why are you crying?"). And it is for this reason that gloom permeates the scene in the manner the witch of a mosquito's itch soon commands one's entire attention. We are witnessing something that is reserved for an individual in his loneliness, something that we cannot possibly share, at the same time as this solitude divulges an area where the person loses his individuality and no longer can be distinguished with any degree of obviousness or comfort. As in the case of Chryses's tears, we can assume, guess . . . suppose . . . even speculate and hypothesize . . . the entire business to which we devote ourselves daily as hermeneuts of other people's tics or temperaments. In contrast to the priest, however, Achilles does not detach himself from the community, like a Sunday from its surrounding week, in order to vent feelings, sentiments, or even particularly fervent thoughts, but to mine them and mull them over. What he is contemplating is as little known to us as to his own mother. Placed in the margin of epic action, like a supplement easily overlooked, the passage both is and is concerned with a zone of emotion for which no expression is suited beyond the silent, saline clamation of tears. At most:

> I feel how the gray time draws through me.
> It hollows me out.
> I feel how the gray time draws through me.

And:

> For a long time I have been dreaming back.
> I dream myself gray down in the gray depth.

This, if anything, is the starting point of solitude. By the "gray" sea Achilles is solitaire. For this kind of loneliness, so free of spectral colors but still so spectral, so anonymous and blank yet so densely distinguished, for this kind of loneliness so fundamental that it lacks speech, shade, and sharpness, for this loneliness about which nothing can be said, asserted, or assumed without thereby forfeiting its most essential trait, which is its solitude, for this loneliness only one activity is possible and solely one act will do: to dream oneself into the gradual, gradual depth of the ocean . . . ingrained . . . like "gray in gray," as Hegel saw it. Thus for this kind of solitude, so gaunt and lonely it possesses no marks of recognition, yet so instantly recognizable it seems in no need of any, for in this loneliness exists only one pattern . . . one figure . . . or, well, one form: the purely pressed discharge of tears that is always plural.

"For a long time already, I had experienced an uncanny, even fearful feeling," Adelbert von Chamisso has his hero—or, rather, anti-hero—Schlemihl echo after he has sold his shadow to the "quaint gray man." *Mir war . . . graulich zumute . . .* This is the feeling, or better: experience, we would like to wrap our words around like a blanket cast across the shoulders of that solitary figure performing his hunchbacked wanderings along wild, misty shores. Mellow and uncanny, tinged with dread and unease: *graulich*. Sensing its felty touch, we become acutely aware of ourselves—as if another person, gray of course, suddenly had sprouted up inside us.

In *The Invention of Solitude,* a book of much mellow ardor, much gentle candor, there is a section where this "grayening"—let us call it—receives formulation. In its second half, entitled "The Book of Memory," the text's anonymous narrator, "A.," is visiting Amsterdam. Lying alone on the bed, he is "idly looking through a guide book he found." A hotel room. And thus loneliness. Thus anonymity. Hence A. "For no particular reason," on the spur of the moment, A. decides to visit the Anne Frank museum. It happens on that most abandoned day of the week that is its first and last, the day for rest and reflection, and he walks there on empty streets:

> It was a Sunday morning, gray with rain, and the streets along the canal were deserted. He climbed the steep and narrow staircase inside the house and entered the secret annex. As he stood in Anne Frank's room, the room in which the diary was written, now bare, with the faded pictures of Hollywood movie stars she collected still pasted to the walls, he suddenly found himself crying. Not sobbing, as might happen in response to a deep inner pain, but crying without sound, the tears streaming down his cheeks, as if purely in response to the world.

Here, too, a gray and deserted day; here, too, an area separated from the rest of the world; and here, too, the protected/protracted/procured space in which a lonely body is breathing and moving about, letting the thoughts it harbors sift, shift, and stray through the mind.

Four walls and a small door, little more, perhaps a window and some cut-out magazine pictures pasted to the walls in memory of the world outside. This is "the room in which the diary was written." Said to be the confidant of the lonely brooder, the diary does not permit us to share our loneliness, however (although we may address it as "Dear Diary" or even "You"), as much as it is the medium in which our solitude becomes conscious of itself—and thus reveals itself to be something separating us from ourselves, articulating an inner divide like the timber in the thudding course of train tracks . . . or in the words of *A Mölna Elegy*, a text spoken by a batch of disembodied huffs of voice:

> Brooding, brooding, and brooding
> until you have brooded yourself double
> on both then and now
> both one and two.
> Then your waiting is over:
> something gray stands by your side,
> that which in the end is you.

If faith is put in Gunnar Ekelöf's poem, much in the way our trust is poured into a handshake, the result of brooding on questions of self and certainty is "something gray"—like that light, cool, clear mist that was spreading on a window pane one day in February when a boy, turning ten, stood stamping with runny nose and burning ear lobes, waiting for his best (only) friends, two immigrant brothers, to open the kitchen door, so the three could play dice as previously arranged. It was the sixth day of the month, a Sunday, and it was his birthday. Impatience itched the boy's body as the sticky cap his head (his hair already stirred into a burrow of moisture) and it was then—there and then—that he understood for the first time the word "solitude." Neither seemed, nor thought to grasp, but understood. Understood without the shade of a doubt and as immovable as the rock on which disbelief cannot be cast. Yes . . . there was . . . is . . . dizziness in that realization, and because of the dizziness a difficulty in breathing, and because of the sudden shortness of breath a feeling of wanting . . . well . . . to happen outside of oneself. As if the ten-year old's solitude had seeped into the steam spreading on the window pane with the red-striped curtain hanging inside: a vapor of finest individuation that his own panting alone could confirm, but which was thus also as fleeting as breathing itself, volatile yet unerring, a batch of mist materializing his breath while concealing the facial reflection in the glass.

I and me.

A solitude, then, grayening, which confirms its detachment by suspending all imagery in dampest indistinction. Hovering oxygen molecules spreading their cover of humidity in the name of disappearance. Even more: as if loneliness could appear only by vanishing and the emergence of tears was its only correlate. Here . . . yes, only here: "tears streaming down his cheeks, as if purely in response to the world." And thus:

> It was at that moment, he later realized, that The Book of Memory began. As in the phrase: "she wrote her diary in this room."

For it is only in loneliness that the work of memory can commence, and for him, the ten-year old boy with the cap, it began outside, looking for a way out.

So. So although the diary offers a method to attain—a way to maintain—solitude, to recall it at the moment it is perceived, it does not provide a safe in which to secure the wonders of interiority, but rather exposes the I to itself. This experience, simultaneously discovery and destruction, invention and ruin, we propose to call a "nostalgia for the present," and since it confers and effaces distinction at the same time, it remains gray for us . . . like rubbery granules of eraser or dreams of denser dreams . . . the drowsy ticking of clocks not set properly . . . or ~~words struck out~~ . . . gray, yes, gray and crumbling and austere.

Like Achilles, the person who writes not a diary, but let us call it . . . well . . . a "day book" . . . remember . . . the person who writes a day book is always more and less than himself, as he appears in a light that emanates neither as the crisp and brilliant double housed in a mirror, nor swims dissolved in the warm yolk of a desk lamp, but emerges rather from the difference between these alternatives, a source mistier than light but clearer than darkness, as gray as air shuffled into a shoe box. Such a book cannot be of the kind from which Gide constructed a persona regardless of how private he wanted to appear, nor does it involve confessions of the careful sort that Augustine or Rousseau put on paper. It contains neither the unadulterated reflections Thoreau wrote with implements provided by the family factory (Emerson: "in his pocket: diary and pencil"), nor the splendid insincerities Henry James took down in a notebook used like a smithy in which he tested the fineness of words and suppleness of phrase. Rather it is a gray concoction of time-space wad, contained within covers as fleeting as fog, in which the distance between I and me is measured and examined, groping for expression like the thief for silver cutlery hidden among the folded sheets and moth balls in a closet . . . a sheath, then, or rather a shell, a vessel in which a legion of voices susurrates, lying, plying, and multiplying, withering, shaking, and deteriorating . . . and finally always hollowed out. If there were a record in Mark's gospel of the grumble of the swine rushing headlong down a precipice into the sea, this might be it. Falling and rising. Then rising. Falling and rising. Then falling. Only falling.

No dust jacket, then, wrapping a volume kept as a sanctuary in which to cloister one's self, but a book of dust and depletion. A threshold essay, so to speak, filled with vapor and voices. Turn to it and pray for safe crossing. This is a gray book.

The only condition required for such a tome, or so it seems, is that far-off tremble, that sliver of a shiver prior to *fiat*, anterior to commencing, which compels it toward its proper beginning and thus ensuing demise:

> In that it is a thing that will forever escape understanding, he wants it to stand for him as the thing that will always come before the beginning. As in the sentences: "This is where it begins. He stands alone in an empty room and begins to cry."

The empty room. Or: everything's beginning. Then stirrings, so stillness, then the twin terrors of life and letters. And therefore tears.

Possessing neither definition nor clarity, these tears are no more than vaguaries, to coin a word, recalling, as if from some remote relay of mnemonic being, the window we passed almost every day during an entire summer more than twenty years after that Sunday in February in front of the kitchen window: in the morning on the way to the local library, the park, or, usually, one of the cafés, or late in the afternoon returning to our temporary lodgings a few flights up. Located on the first floor in a yellow two-story house dating from the turn of the century, it faced the backyard with its fire-wall and the windows were always kept open but the blinds remained shut. Or almost. For these blinds, we imagined, were slanted just slightly, like the brim of a hat, so that the room could catch a bit of the summer's changing radiance, darkness, and whatever motions stirred the dusk between the poles of light and night. A place to which the day came only in slits of gaze.

In this room . . . No. Wait. Lost again. Where were we? What was the purpose of fondling this bit of memory-tissue, pulled out of a pocket of nothingness? O. Yes. The analogy. Well, this is it—and it is not much: we thought that the gray space-time we imagined preceded all beginning could be recreated thus: windows ajar, blinds pulled, facing the backyard, with nobody there. This large cool cell, gray as only our sullen imagination would paint it . . . with its, we guessed, single chair and desk, perhaps a carelessly made bed that looked more like a cot or a stretcher, some newspapers piled in a corner, and two or three long candles, drifting dust balls, an empty glass, not much more . . . perhaps a small saucer doing service as an ashtray, a few cigarette butts, and a couple of doves on the window sill demanding attention (but if anything only startling the room's shadows that now fluttered homelessly across the walls) . . . we imagined that this empty room contained nothing but absence—absence, light, and the transient shades of luminous lack—or what Clov in *Endgame* wrapped up in two words spanning an entire universe between them: "light black. From pole to pole."

And thus nothing.

What was it that so enticed us in this space-time? What caused us, every time we went up- or downstairs (we lived on the second floor and had to make two loops, like the folded figure of an eight, around the shaft containing the elevator, which was out of order, which had not worked for as long as we could remember, not since we visited the house for the first time as a child a few years old at most, which perhaps had not functioned since the war—"the last" as they said where we were), what caused us to feel *relieved* by this anonymous site, abandoned, it seemed, like a flat tire?

It could not simply be the fact that the backyard was a paradise of gray colors . . . strange contradiction . . . with its charcoal cement wall on the off side, the slightly lighter yard, also cemented but now covered with gravel, the garbage cans made of galvanized plate, the gray sheet metal, and the white window sills that in the course of time had turned gray, too, from rain, snow, and insidious particles of carbon monoxide (not remaining invisible when collected in sufficiently large quantities, but covering things with a dull sheet of dirt that first became a thin film, but finished by solidifying into a crust as thick as cake frosting) . . . no . . . no . . . not that. Even if it were because of this gray paradise that we felt relieved and experienced the odd pleasure of breathing, it could not provide the only reason for the light dizziness we always sensed, the abandon that seized us without slightest fail, so similar to the feeling we had confused with annoyance more than twenty years earlier.

Now, at a distance that is nothing to speak of, we believe it must have had to do with the fact that the room demonstrably existed, open yet closed, and that it thus encouraged us to imagine things only as settings that could not be beheld. It contained a presence impossible to gauge, interfused with the shuffle of shade and absence to which we were treated. Like a breathless *O* from a gaping mouth. And that was what gray was for us: an invisible presence. So . . . so this was the way it had to be, too, we figured, in the cage clause sanctum in which we would orient ourselves along that lively lead. Our epoch of grayening. (Still not closed.)

It is high time, now, to account for the texture of this unknown something, our sullen, glorious "it." If grayness is an indefinition emerging like that past breath on a window pane, it would seem, would it not, we might trace its contours only in the act in which we experience vagueness. In a text about "Unknowing, Laughter, and Tears," which we came across during the summer mentioned, Georges Bataille waved on a few suggestions in this direction. Only two things are certain, he claimed: we do not know everything and we are going to die. Thus "an insufferable void" is uncovered in the midst of existence, like suddenly the cancerous lump in a breast. When a human being says: "I am ashamed of having wanted to be everything, for I see now that it was to sleep," as Bataille had pointed out already in the text chronicling his *expériénce intérieure*, this thought opens up an abyss. From now on the person moves in a strange world where "anguish and ecstasy" permeate each other. Attempting to provide the existential grammar for this experience, he considered it an encounter with the unknown.

During afternoons as hot as a baker's armpits, we copied passages from this book as well as from his essay on laughter and tears, among them one in which Bataille mentions "the unknown's sudden invasion" in a person's life, arguing that "it is impossible to talk about this unknown except in the moment of experiencing it." While laughter is characterized by a dominating attitude toward the unknown, the passage continued, tears possess "a fundamental ambiguity":

> Everybody knows that it is wonderful to weep, that tears provide a kind of consolation that in fact a person often does not want to accept but that is overwhelming.

Unlike laughter, which provides a jubilant triumph over the unknown, tears imply the floating submission to it. But this distinction is still drawn too sharply, Bataille underlines, because suspended certainty may be found in both cases:

> There is something gray in tears, in the same way as there is something gray in laughter. I do not think it would be difficult to demonstrate that both tears and laughter are connected with the invasion of the unknown, with the suppression of that part of the world that we consider as known .... If a person dies, for example, the fact is that our known order is changed in a fundamental way, and that we are forced to see ourselves (in front of us, despite ourselves) substitute

what we know with something we do not know—for example the presence of a dead person, or more precisely formulated: the absence of the living. More than anything else, tears mark disappearance, the sudden destruction of the known world to which we belong.

Il y a quelque chose de grisant.... Tears, then, as the passive confirmation of the unknown. Marking something that is in the process of losing itself, they affirm a dispersal gradually or suddenly emerging. The "absence of the living." And thus gray. For what is it that floats away, runs out, and is destroyed, squandered, and liquidated in the mollified element of tears? Nothing but the known. But also: nothing less.

Still, tears can be of many kinds, and the known does not always have to be the same. We may imagine, for example, the different tears caused by suffering and grief respectively, the former plump like ripe rolling berries and the latter thin as the strings on a violin; then there are the bitter tears of loathing and despair, to be sure, false tears lacking the salt of dignity, and agonizing tears hot as wax; there are the dammed-up tears of the sublime and the chilling ones cold as corpses; but also the tears of bliss and wonder that tremblingly unite rather than separate, the crocodile's tears, and the soppy secretions of insinuation; there are those tears that merely amount to dry drizzles of exhaustion and those that in hot torrents release their helpless subject from stinging humiliation; and then, of course, there are the tears that dangle like commas on the verge of abandoning one line's gutter in order to fall toward the next, then at some point silently receding, with willful abandon, further down the page.

The *vallis lacrimarum* of the Bible and Vergil's thoughts on "the tears of things" may be counted among the vocabulary of crying (like the latter's name when our eyes are grumbled), but also the tears that are said to be the sign of God's grace (*donum lacrimarum*), to which we may add the many stations on a child's repertoire, ranging from wary sobs and annoying whimpers caused by concentrated fatigue, to uncontrollable downpours without rhyme and reason (as if crying were an art in itself). "Oh, my love," exclaims a certain Sineusov (artist),

I bite my knuckles so as not to start shaking with sobs, but there is no holding them back; down I slide with locked brakes, making "hoo" and "boohoo" sounds, and it is all such humiliating physical nonsense: the hot blinking, the feeling of suffocation, the dirty handkerchief, the convulsive yawning alternating with the tears—I just can't, can't live without you.

For, yes, of course, there is that, too: the mindless spasms that rack us when love first dislocates, then nimbly removes the reason for our rectitude, pulling it out through the mouth with a twist and a flourish. Such spineless, amorous idiocy. And then there are the wet pillows caused by hearts squeezed with cruel indifference and there are the touching trembles of compassion; there are the sudden eruption in a long awaited reunion and the warm wetness of reconciliation; there are Isolde's tears over Tristan and Werther's hot pearls of precious pain.

Young developed an entire "philosophy of tears" in his *Night Thoughts*—

> *A tear!*—can tears suffice?—but not for me.
> How vain our efforts! and our arts how vain!

—and in *Flegeljahre*, Jean Paul talked about the handkerchief, this inevitable object, this obliging cloth utensil, as a "tear-sign," whereas Gottfried Keller thought that cheeks became much too soft much too often in Jean Paul, pointing out that his romantic colleague ordered "too many hemorrhages of tears and blood" for his heroes. And so on in never ceasing streams . . . for tears are as numerous as a mother's admonitions, as manifold as the whirling loops on fingertips . . . as countless as the tongues of Legion.

Most objective—most sarcastic—Hans Castorp must be when he witnesses Joachim's death in *The Magic Mountain*:

> Later also he stood weeping, the tears washed over his cheeks . . . , this clear liquid that flows so abundantly and so bitterly throughout the world and at every hour of the day that it has provided the poetic name for the valley of the earth. This alkaline-salty product of the glands that is pressed out of our body through joltings of the nerves

and penetrating pain, both physical and mental. He knew that it also contained some mucin and albumin.

The last sentence offers a version of Bataille's example and has the same effect as a red-eyed look in an unexpected mirror. Eyes staring at staring eyes.

If laughter is the art of action, tears are the mild element of passion. Steam, fog, and dew: the emotive goose-bumps for things cared for. But also river, valley, sea: the seemingly inexhaustible reservoirs from which oil is tapped to soothe pain and torment. In contrast to the resounding outburst of laughter, as phallic as a naked sword, tears present a more pliable eruption. As Quintilian pointed out in the *Institutio Oratoriae*, their source are the eyes, whereas laughter installs itself in the mouth. Among the verbs that Latin, for example, exhibits—*flere, plorare, heiulare, lamentare, vagire*—none epitomizes more tellingly the mild, yet quiescently coercive character of tears than *ululare*. To taste the word is to experience how it sticks in a throat thick with hesitation, *huh*, before it begins to disentangle itself, *uh huh*, from its shelter of shyness, eking out of its reserve, and then begins to roll on, *uh huh huh*, without rein or restraint... *uh huh huhlare*... *uh huh hulare*... (Quick image of scrawny cogwheels on which, one by one, the eye's warm drops of amber oil are falling.)

A choking eulogy to chance.

That this eruptive occasion may be not only impassioned or uncalled for, but occasionally also quite candidly embarrassing, is indicated by several texts, but none as well as Klopstock's *Messiah*, weeping's uncrowned apogee, in which lament is accentuated by exclamation marks as demonstrative as a herald's announcing staff:

> Israel stepped forward in triumph! and the soul full of tears, thankful tears streaming down from the resurrected's eyes: hallelujah to the conqueror of death!

Here are no commas rolling cautiously from gutters, only full periods hurled down as if they were comic strip bombs with sputtering fuses. (If roughness be the name of the game, we would prefer the kind found some hundred years earlier, for example in a medieval ballad in which lamentation is described as a "bursting of the heart and splitting of the skull." Sentimentality must be countered with dry aplomb.)

Yet what social psychologists call "the lacrimal discharge" need not always appear as accommodating and compliant, quiet quietly submissive. The most precious tears, at any rate, fluid discharges more valuable than amber yet weighing less than air, are those that prevent a person from speaking—are tokens of lament only to the extent that they render language impossible without therefore replacing it. Sticking, stuttering, blockage. Tears, that is, as that the French call *points de suspension*, ellipsis or omission, a trinity of dots causing language to halt, representing, as has been remarked in memory of L. I. Shigaev, "the foot-prints of words that have departed on tiptoe." The gray dominion of interruption.

Examples abound. In order to keep the eyes glossy with unshed tears, however, we shall examine only one sample before moving on to our next element, dry as sand left lying in the sun. Consider "La Jeune parque," a text in which the past casually/continually leaks into the present like rain through a poorly shingled roof. "Whence born?," Valéry asks in his poem,

> What labor ever solemn and new
> Draws you with delay, tear, from the bitter shadow?

Although tardiness characterizes the element in which the "young fate" lives, the "labor" performed by its tear is always new—and thus can belong only to the delayed Now under which it is suffering. (Another nostalgia for the present.) Then:

> In the time in which I live your long delays
> Stifle me . . . Silent, I drink your steady course . . .

No matter how long the pause might be in which language is suspended in the poem's three points—creating that strangely delayed present proper only to grayening (*les lenteurs que tu fais / M'étouffent . . .*)—a trembling ellipsis immediately indicates the new arrival of tears and thereby again a postponement as well as a cessation of language (*Je me tais, buvant ta marche sûre*...). Before its arrival, Valéry's *larme* literally strangles language; when it finally arrives, it forces it into silence.

In gray areas, we would thus like to end by proposing, language seems to exist only during the period when it appears between the tear's delay... and arrival. Yet this is the very space of time in which it is interrupted, too, breaking into the three dots that mark its beginning and end. For Valéry's young fate, stuck in a zone of vagueness, language is first a remnant and last a suggestion. Its Now is always Not-yet or No-more. As impossible to catch as a mosquito in darkness. Either we are already suffering from its effects or we are worried about its itching sting soon to come. Either way, we live in the present only to the degree that we cannot tolerate it. *Uns wird graulich zumute.*

Could this painful Neithernor be but gray... pricking, running, tearing, piercing as when our hand pecks the pencil's point against the plane of paper... making it shake and crumble... writhing... and cease?

> I feel how the gray time draws through me.
> It has drawn through me already for a long time.
> It hollows me out.
> It bleaches my dreams.
> I tremble and shake.
> I crumble.

§ Two

Crumbling and decaying, grayening, then, amounts to acts of disappearance: when window panes are scraped clean of their crystal crust or the gramophone needle slides out of its shallow groove with a thick screech followed by a wailing thud (before landing on a spinning island of paper and hype); when wind catches our umbrella with a gusto sudden as a surge of voltage or coins roll into dusty corners, placidly pirouetting themselves into place in cushioned darkness; when shades mingle and gases oxidize; when weary gravel whirls with limber air, smoke sets itself free from fire, or rugs are beaten with muffled anger; when cold drafts clear bedrooms with swift, clean clout on February mornings; when rideaux of rain—these sad-streaked raiments—push by like cardboard settings on a stage; when it gets to be early and when it begins to be late; when the cat, privy to mysteries of a different order, follows the drowsy snowflakes outside the window or our hand impatiently spins through the radio channels, only to release static echoes rebounding with enthusiastic inanimation in a vast metallic interior . . . a void of endless voicing . . . yes . . . but also a flurry of gray nullity . . . for gray is when words slide together, and gray is the opulent emptiness we experience when we slowly descend into their teeming confusion, all ears and tears.

So gray must be what we hear, too, when we listen intently to mere "noises, sounds, and sweet aires," those crystalline containers of ether so memorably comprised in *The Tempest*, all phantom limbs and akimbo, timbre, pitch, and delight: the chirping sound of our brass sharpener, for example, when it ganglingly feeds on the yellow finish and sweet wood held in hands no less lank, sending charcoal dust and shavings soundlessly spinning into ethereal non-existence the way we all must go; or the silence of fearful steps, jittery as jelly, lingering on thresholds like breaths caught in the nick of time; squeaking floors or the sudden bicker and commotion when the break/spell/respite is over; the coarse clearing of throats getting unclogged the way pipes are aired or the dry huff of impotence when vacuum cleaners get stuck to resilient mats; the steady clatter of busy signals only telephones give off, radiator crackle, or the cold rattle of keys in coat pockets, reminiscent of distant but still chilling memories . . . all these aerial affairs, easy and limpid, also belong to what words do when words are sunken into. Syllables can change though all the letters will remain; meanings may shift and fade, veering off like streetlights, without the means of telling following suit; and biddings, too, can acquire another edge while their scope and aim stay the same . . . so gray . . . well . . . when gray has us descend into the world within words, clicking and glittering like tiny wheels of a watch encased in glass and enamel, chance will mimic choice and flux be the game of the name.

Which is to say that gray is not only transience, turn, or mutation, but also the rickety skeleton that stubbornly stays when meaning and matter have disintegrated, fat and flesh worn away, and only bones and resilience remain what they always were . . . For gray is the framework, too, of things finite. But is it then both action and structure, transport and stay, tick and—well—tow? As if time, while indeed passing, were also detained, even fortified, in its disappearance? Oh, it would be no more odd than the presence of yeast in dough or a headache pill first freshly sparkling, then vanishing with a thin, gaseous fizzle in a glass of water, leaving only rotations of unexplored orbits behind. Or the effervescence in our throat afterward. The dry foam on the lips. Or the trail of smoke, for that matter, which inertly swings downward, almost like the tablet's dust as it sinks toward the bottom, before coming to a peaceful rest at the precise moment when its disappearance is, why, here. Gray is thus a remnant of itself, it would seem, sputtering and spattering, or silently falling, subdued and chaste, its own gentle disintegration, yet always also a grainy rest . . . this remnant of disappearance . . . that trace of erosion . . . a point whose vanishing gradually turns from verb into noun.

Let us investigate this transformation from act to fact. There is a word for it, or more precisely: a verb. While, in a manner of speaking, it has not yet been born (that is, not yet been delivered by the midwife hands of the *Oxford English Dictionary*), it does feature—phantomatically—for example in Beckett:

> Watt saw, in the grate, of the range, the ashes gray. But they turned pale red, when he covered the lamp, with his hat. The range was almost out, but not quite. A handful of dry chips and the flames would spring, merry in appearance, up the chimney, with an organ note. So Watt busied himself, a little while, covering the lamp, less and less, more and more, with his hat, watching the ashes grayen, redden, grayen, redden, in the grate, of the range.

To "grayen," thus.

Among the mysteries of linguistics is a term that expresses a change of state—the inchoative verb—and we would like to pull it into the scope of our mind. It will provide the slim, short-lived stem (still mostly yellow it seems) on which grayening alone can blossom. "Become" or "begin" are inchoative auxiliary verbs, indicating the task that words of this profession have in common: initiators, they are all transitory. As suggested by other such verbs, like "redden," "grow pale," or "fall asleep," they lack proper extension, like thinking devoid of object, for, we may ask, how long can cheeks redden before we begin to believe we are no longer faced with an embarrassed friend, but with an equally awkward truth: he is too attached to the bottle? Or how long can we be falling asleep without becoming sleep's subject as well as object, and thus dream about ourselves (hush, halt) first liltingly tilting, then (go) thuddingly tumbling into mindlessness? Which is to say that despite initiating a transitory stage the verb also suggests an ending—and one none too uncertain, at that. Much like a mute fuse lit with a sizzle of resignation.

Yes, to grayen, thus. A dictionary would inform us that the verb does in fact exist in a remote Swedish dialect (*gråda*) where it signifies the rippling of water by wind—suddenly, strikingly—without poise, peace, or both. An act with hardly any duration and certainly no permanence. Nonetheless, let us try to behold it, this oddity of a doing, and have it describe an action when such can only be commenced and resumed, again and anew, but neither brought to continue nor to ensue, like water once stirred is water twice moved and thus never . . . ever . . . no, no . . . the same. Its beginning already coming to an end, like an emancipated shade succumbing to nightfall, to grayen would be a respite masked as permanence, a grace period dressed up as duration. A moratorium, in short. But also: a tainting of time which, as passive as water, lacks bulk and substance, yet by being exposed to weather and wind is provided with both shape and appearance, albeit *ersatz*-like in solidity. Hence it is only thanks to time that grayening becomes perceptible, we would like to venture, and only thanks to change that it is able to meander into the realm of the perceptible, like Invisible Man's arms pulling into a pullover.

We want to suggest that the process that time undergoes between the points used to indicate its passing, but especially the time belonging to solitude, be designated thus: a "grayening." It would be a process which, like Watt's silent stirrings, constantly resumes and steadily ceases; it would begin in order to end and end by beginning; it would emerge, that is, by disappearing—and thus also be a noun-turning verb. It is solely during this vanishing act that the I can appear as subject of its own thought . . . in trails of vapor, billow, and gas, for example . . . or steam as steady as a pulse . . . as voluble as the thin, silvery quiver of exquisite nonexistence we experience when we stamp in air having assumed the staircase had another step or two. The feeling never lasts; is an ethereal miracle; and silkily grounded in absence.

Still, it is an "I" who experiences it and experiences it at the very moment that foothold is lost—as for example in the dozing off during a hazy afternoon in the deep verdant shade in the garden of a restaurant in a major city that shall remain unnamed. The thick folios of magnificent trees protect us against the sun's clarifications of a scenario we must continue to keep sufficiently obscure. We lean back in the folding chair, all ease, satin, and repose, closing our eyes on dark, silent well-being. But it is not the images that now slowly begin to appear for the inner vision, as if thawing into existence, that mark the grayening. Nor is it the lazy numbing of limbs, the soothing weight of relaxing muscle and sinew, or the speechless repose presently gathering in the smooth back of the head, but rather the moment when we sink into the semblance of sleep "as such," as philosophers put it, in the midst of susurrating voices, soft detonations of laughter, and erratic sounds from distant cars, dithering flies dotting about, or the occasional leg of a metal chair grinding in gravel . . . when we quite simply disappear while simultaneously remaining entirely present, aware not so much of the other guests' gestures, movements, expressions, as of the atmospheres in which they dwell with such quiet relish, they too leisurely leaning back in their chairs, breaking bread on which soft butter is spread, or smoking cigarettes without filter, recently married, perhaps, yes, still warm from that first surprise at firm expansion of heart, she with his hand in hers, against her cheek, against the lips, her laughter and cajoling, and suddenly we are the mild rush of his blush as he amorously whispers her name—only to realize, with a jerk sudden and unwilled, as if a palm had been turned over or head had become tail, how far we have removed ourselves from presence and purpose, our ears now buzzing, our eyes now dazzled, and a mild drowsiness rapidly clearing behind our frontal lobe like a pit when light is poured into it by the bucket. The couple left long ago and the waiters, busily collecting dishes and bottles, throw us looks mildly annoyed . . . for it is within this distance between here and there, notion and emotion, sunflecked dizziness and migratory mirages of thought, that we find grayening's intoxicating stay and strange extension. Such sunny nonsense. There in the verdant shade, here on the backlit screen of inner vision. Between I and me. Gray. Yes, gray. Yet entirely luminous.

Grayening considered as action is something as odd, thus, too, as an occurrence without proper event, a happening so-called without real deed. The only thing that occurs in its interim, involuntarily as an unmastered sigh, is . . . well . . . "it" . . . which is not much . . . not much of anything . . . not much more than a placeholder, in fact, standing in for something that will never quite acquire shape, not even in the way of inchoate breath emerging from the deeper recesses of the lungs or in the contours of speech when words are supplanted with a gesture, then a laugh and perhaps the shudder of a shoulder. Yet without us noticing it, it finds its ways to occur—tacitly and discreetly, a paragon of neutrality.

"It happened at this time . . . "

"It was said that . . . "

"It was a dark and stormy night . . . "

Consider the anonymous "it" in these ways to begin a story (as worn as train rails, we must admit, but reliable for getting us where we want). It is entirely decisive, as no one surely would wish to dispute, the backbone of any body of work, the *sine qua non* of storytelling no less, since it constitutes the only available—albeit fragile—link to the When in which what happened took place (a life buoy sort of, attached to a sewing thread). Yet it remains so discreet that it resembles more the careful crease in a gentleman's pants than our telling's clearing a trek through the regions of a story. Consider it. Does it not constitute something that we take for granted, but do not heed until it is gone, reported missing, turned absent? like the unfounded trust our knee places in the phantomatic twelfth step in a staircase that can claim only eleven? Well? So much for transcendence.

Similarly, we use "it" in order to determine or ask something. "It is raining," we may say, for example, with dry annoyance perhaps or a neutral pitch, or "How is it going?," the voice quickly rubbed warm, now heading in the direction of noncommittal benevolence. And we assume that we know what "it" is when we say it, and what we mean to say is that it, the word "it," stands for something that need not be said, or something that cannot be said. But if the thing we say is something that eludes us, something we do not understand, how can we persist in saying that we understand what we are saying? And yet it goes without saying that we do. The "it," for example, in the preceding sentence, "it goes without saying," is in fact nothing less than whatever it is that propels us into the act of speech itself. And if it, the word "it," is what continually recurs in any effort to define it, then it must be accepted as the given, the precondition of the saying of it.

It is just that: it. Like smoke without fire it is given yet remains unfathomable, and like fumes released with ornamental care from pillar-formed cigarettes it is so gray that it need not be defined more precisely as something that "is" and is "gray" when it is what it is. It is simply "given," as Paul Auster remarks in the passage our eyes just combed through. That sober crease in the flannel, that wilted cessation, a fold of thinnest nil.

Providing nothing to hang, clasp, or hold on to, it nevertheless leaves a trail. For, as Auster continues to point out, and our paraphrase would like to confirm, in order to observe it as "it" another it is required—yet this second "it" demands its own it in turn, and so on in a series of hoops as fine and fragile as rings of smoke. Or the loops of locution delicately traced when *a rose is a rose is a rose*. In order to be truly taken stock of, "it" must be determined as something else, each faint ring thus referring to the next . . . zero-shaped subtleties with no lasting meaning of their own, feeble ventures of a gray mouth strung together purely by the audio-oral dance of chance . . . that, well, makes us rather suspect that (gray) telling must be in the (indirect) showing, merely a transition from one paper-thin "it" to the one following, between it and the "it" that it is, tremblingly spreading out and gradually vanishing like wreaths on drugged water.

Understood in this manner, by repercussion so to speak, grayening would be what makes time readable: shaky circles penciled on sheets of air or scratched on the flat face of the sea, expanding wrinkily only to merge with the oblivion on which they were once written, merely marking the monument of a momentary ripple, a transient trans, a crease first unfolding, then ceasing to be. Although such grayening may provide form for the formless, it seems itself thus to appear only by being attached to something else, like an escaping trail of effervescent dizziness, the elastic, colorless gauze swaddled around an invisible body of air. A vanishing turning point.

Plaster for phantom limbs.

Imagine now that the opposite of water and wind mingling could be examined by running it through a miniscule, derelict projector mounted on a tripod in the gentle darkness at the back of our head. Find a seat, adjust to the silent humming of the celluloid, then observe a tin soldier projected on the verso of the fronthead. First stout and sturdy, all pledge and allegiance, he now . . . o . . . he now gradually—no, oh, he now rapidly begins to melt in the crackling embrace of a fire we had initially taken to be tongues of snow, licks of ice, twisted, turned, and deformed by heated imagination. No liquid here, then, no, neither tears, nor water, but only flame, blister, and migration. Granted, an added touch of distant red may stain the screen (like in *Watt*), or a lingering waft of some gruesome gridelin (as in the drowner's lead-colored lips, for example), but the point of the inversion may still be made: grayening is not confined to the element of water, our first matter, but can also occur in its fiery contrast. For to smolder, smoke, or belch are transitory processes, too, without duration or stability, starting again for every new fiber of wood consumed, and beginning to cease therefore as soon as they are ignited, be it by fire or fancy.

Considered each other's diametrical opposites, water and fire are elements whose symbolic status has been combined with assorted body fluids, seasons, and temperaments ever since Theofrastus first attempted to define differences of human disposition in the *Problemata*. But even if melancholy normally is associated with black bile and fall, hence correlated with earth rather than water, it is not merely ruled by depression's law of gravity, but can also—as in Klopstock—become an element of fluidity. And though fire is said to be crackling and choleric, it does not lack relation to air; a certain weightless anger, perhaps, light and tight like breath on a cold day in February. Which is to say that elements may be yoked—water and earth can be brought together, just as fire and air may unite—demonstrating not only similar tendencies or matching inclinations, but also that elements can assume characteristics different from those traditionally ascribed to them. If tears exhibit the melancholic's temperament in fluid form, say, vapor could be the result of the choleric's belching resentment.

Eustache Deschamps, the fourteenth-century poet, once wrote a variegation of verses entitled "Je doy estre chancelliers des Fumeux." In its mildly ironic manner, the poem offers us further direction to the act and fact of grayening, as it outlines a figure, all pluvial and sibilant sigh, whose facial traits we slowly begin to make out and recognize, albeit with fumes still smudging the grasp of our gaze. Announcing our second element—raise the finger called Finger for short—the poem could be rewritten thus in free and unkempt English:

> I must remain the chancellor of Vapor
> And forever at work.
> I make an effort to maintain order,
> Because one does not always find me
> In the same condition, but rather sees certainty
> Suddenly change to illusion,
> First sad and then happy.
> Then I vanish like smoke, often inclined
> To brood, yet without knowing why.
>
> By nature I am melancholic,
> One might find me downright choleric.
> Yes, by nature I am inclined toward the strange,
> And I must accept it.
> Since it is not possible to change
> I remain filled with great melancholy,
> For I am not able to afford resistance.
> Strength for that is lacking. Often it disposes me
> Toward brooding, without knowing why.

> If I am rarely seen happy I excuse myself
> By pointing to my disposition,
> I am not intelligent enough to know
> How I might counteract my own nature.
> Enveloped in smoke I must thus pass
> My life in fumes and continue to work.
> You will always find me in this condition,
> Inclined to brood without knowing why.

Only neatness and duty provide Deschamps's fragile figure with the necessary stability in life, a stalk-like body on which imagination is presently doing its best to shape a familiar face with some hardening smoke and a sponge-full of forgetting. But better leave it alone, on second thought, like the gaseous flimsy of a spirit stuck in its bottle. To give the figure shape would amount to removing that security known as the cork. We would not want to do that. Not yet.

As secretary in a ministry of mist, Deschamps's grayening character must maintain a sense of measure, proportion, and structure, brooding without finding a satisfactory answer to the flits of imagination that wrenches its brain like snaky twists of sleep may a dormant arm. From this perspective it is not difficult to understand why the melancholic often has been accused not only of vaporish dispensations, but also of a *manie de perfection*, that need bordering on insanity to find a place and order for everything, especially his own shapeless pondering. The melancholic broods himself double with trouble—"bottled up," as the saying goes (jamming down the cork without further ado)—so instead of releasing this frail figure into a world of future worry, let us first take heart, then a closer look at what is being tapped and enclosed therewithin . . . for our chosen color may be nothing more than this: flightiness in temporary custody.

As Pandora's box of fright and terror can be handled only with the lid carefully placed and sealed, so the spirit in the oil lamp can be controlled only if the cover is not polished and the hood of the pipe remains in place—roughly in the same way Strindberg is said to have kept the sou'wester on his head after the daily morning walk, so ideas and impressions fretting like popcorn would not abscond during his subsequent work at the desk. But what happens, not when the lamp is polished or the box opened, but inside? What happens under the cork, the cap, the hood, the lock? What is the life like of dashing spirits and thousand torments when they are *not* accessible, enveloped in whirling billow and harangues of haze, hitting gray foreheads against the no less gray insides of their container? And—yes, not to forget—what is existence like in any unknown space or room, but first and foremost the one contained in what we have referred to as "this"?

Few texts describe such an existence better than "The Fall of the House of Usher," first published in September 1839, in a journal with such a dampened gray title, *Burton's Gentleman's Magazine*, that cigar smoke and rattling newspapers still cling to its name. In this story of despair and decay, melancholy takes on its grayest form, if nothing else because "it" here assumes a guise even more gruesome than that of death. Poe's short story is an account of heightened sensitivity, phantomlike events, and a secret so gloriously ghastly it seems to defy articulation. The author's clarification in a letter to his friend Griswald, concerning the ballad about a haunted palace that one of the main characters in the story recites by heart, might serve as a description of what happens in this web thick with whisper and anguish: "By 'The Haunted Palace' I mean to imply a mind haunted by phantoms—a disordered brain."

Poe's text has been considered an example of what was once termed *das Unheimliche*, an appraisal we would not wish to dispute here. For Freud, the vehicle of "the uncanny" was repetition: like a revenant, wafer-thin and skittish, proceeding by sudden heaps of movement, it lacked the tactile comfort and soothing intimacy we like to associate with "our" world, all soft yet certain, with a tad of light swimming even in the pupil of darker moments. Still we experience a feeling of recognition when it strikes us, which may imply, as Freud suggested, that the uncanny does not constitute the opposite of what we take to be known or familiar, neatly corresponding as a shady verso to its blank recto, but rather something altogether more warped and unpleasant. *Un-*

heimlich, it belongs to the strange and forlorn, vaguely alarming and always uncertain, like the hissing sound discharged from darkness when light is suddenly extinguished and we are forced to continue with left foot trepidly tapping and arms extended like wobbly sticks into a membranous dead end.

From such and similar occasions emerges an insecurity dully gathering like wad in our minds, only to be suddenly stirred into life when some unintentional repetition adds its uncanny touch to the otherwise harmless number, name, or task, "and forces us to consider the idea of something fated and unavoidable where we otherwise would have talked about 'bad luck.'" Seized with doubt, not knowing what to do with the cottony black hole presently expanding like a blot of ink in our consciousness, we believe we may distinguish a plan, a pattern, a precedent, and thus rush to term this untaught tangle of chance and conjecture "fate" or "kismet" or "destiny" or "doom." It should be clear, however, that the dangerous aspect of this experience is not the meeting with an automated girl with dead eyes or a chessplaying Turk. The uncanny part is that we—indubitably at once—understand that we are ourselves the receptacle in which the experience takes place, containing *das Unheimliche* like a vessel its foreign cargo, without being able to claim it ours. The exterior has long since become part of the interior, we are forced to realize, yet it remains unassimilated and alien, densely flocking like letters to form a cloud in our mind, still instantly falling apart in tidbits of scattered nullity if we try to mold it into shape and cognition.

As Poe's short ballad is contained in the strange story about the fall of the house of Usher, haunting the narrative with the truth it seems incapable of easing into words, so the castle Usher harbors a brain obsessed by a similarly "discordant melody" and even "evil things," afflictions written in crackling script on the horrid face of the building itself. There are wrinkles attesting to old age and too much history, a malaise in all respects counterproductive. The reader approaches this irregularly doubled, peculiarly reflected place along somber roads toward the end of a remote year, in a region long since brushed into oblivion:

> During the whole of a dull, dark, and soundless day in the autumn of the year, when the clouds hung oppressively low in the heavens, I had been passing alone, on horseback, through a singularly dreary tract of country, and at length found myself, as the shades of the evening drew on, within view of the melancholy House of Usher.

Notice how the castle waits to appear within view until we have labored our way through the winding thicket of adjectives . . . *dull, dark, and soundless* . . . twisting and turning under their consonants' catarrhal weight . . . *clouds hung oppressively low in the heavens* . . . at long last reaching the already dark evening and the end of the sentence. Only then: *the melancholy House of Usher*, a final point as heavy as breathing after we have walked—in another life, at a far away place—the distance from beach to home in wet shoes without laces, sand adding injury to insult. Or covered this introductory paragraph. And notice that it is not the narrator who discovers the castle after a day's tiring ride, but rather he who comes within its vision (*found myself . . . within view*)—as if Poe's protagonist merely lets himself be drawn to this gray zone, rather than had been looking for it with a preference for purpose and aim in mind. In this short story, when sufficiently eyed and scrutinized, acting subjects turn out to be passive objects of action.

Lets "himself become drawn," we said, but this would still suggest lingering voluntariness. Poe's anonymous narrator has in fact been called to the castle Usher after having received a letter from its master "which, in its wildly importunate nature," could be answered in no other form than with an immediate visit. Here too, then, there is not much room for decisions based on content or desire. Readiness is all:

> It was the manner in which all this, and much more, was said—it was the apparent *heart* that went with his request—which allowed me no room for hesitation; and I accordingly obeyed forthwith what I still considered a very singular summons.

It was the manner and not the content, the feeling and not the thought. Poe even writes "it was the apparent *heart*"—as if the summons were dictated by a circumstance going to the narrator's seat of empathy and response in such forceful, immediate way it must be obeyed. No. Matter. What. Much could be said about this "apparent *heart*"—especially in light of the story's epigram that claims that *Son coeur est un luth suspendu; / Sitôt qu'on le touche il résonne* ("His heart is a suspended lute; / As soon as it is touched it resonates"). But instead of touching that string already now—and in its suspended tremble listen to the struggle played out between *luth* and *lutte* in Poe's story—at this early point in our perusal of the plot we shall affect a blithe ignorance of its vicissitudes and stress instead "the manner," for the author seems in effect to supply us with a hint of how his text may be read:

> I looked upon the scene before me—upon the mere house, and the simple landscape features of the domain—upon the bleak walls—upon the vacant eyelike windows—upon a few rank sedges—and upon a few white trunks of decayed trees—with an utter depression of soul which I can compare to no earthly sensation more properly than to the afterdream of the reveler upon opium—the bitter lapse into everyday life—the hideous dropping off of the veil.

From color to black-and-white . . . or from pigmented intoxication to unsheltered sobriety. In the same way as trees in February rattle against the horizon without living connection with each other, so Poe introduces dashes in his text in order to stress the depressing isolation that characterizes the gray area entered into by his narrator, experienced as a dingy awakening from the spacious befuddlement of opium fumes—like coming back to one's humdrum body out of languorous, variegated mist.

Yet in Poe's particular case the question is whether it is not an awakening to a reality that is so ghostly it remains a puzzle, a lump of oddity and desolation. The bewitchment does not decrease, we would like to suggest, its character merely changes. Becoming cold and chilling, like the raw heap of fish scales along the blade of a knife, it tears apart the visions' luxurious images, yet does so only to reveal a reality from which life has been whisked away like blood from a face fraught with fright. Poe's seems to be an awakening inside the stupor, or rather on its cold side, a breaking of the illusion that is still under the influence, so to speak, in the same way a dream about awakening does not awaken us but continues to be a dream and part of a dream . . . and thus no return but a continuation . . . without red-rimmed glow and intensity, to be sure, and empty as hollow eye sockets, yet: a continuation. ("It is no longer possible to dream about the blue flower," Benjamin once stated; "The person who today awakens as Heinrich von Ofterdingen has overslept." The sleepy bewitchment of satisfied intoxication—fabulously gathered into a blue flower, the object of all longing and each infinity—is transformed into emptiness, dust, and deterioration. "The dream no longer opens toward a blue distance," Benjamin then dryly concludes; "it has become gray. The gray layer of dust over things is its best part." Such, too, is awakening in Poe: a layered dust.)

Poe's narrator has been summoned to the dismal region in which lives his childhood friend Roderick Usher, the "time-honored" family's youngest descendant and also the castle's last lord. A neurasthenic with high cheek bones and mournful eyes, Usher prevails in a life as worn as the slippers in which he drags it about. But before the narrator is received by a valet and the old friends shake hands, he directs his horse toward "the precipitous brink of a black and lurid tarn that lay in unruffled luster by the dwelling." On this threshold to the story, Poe's narrator contemplates "the mansion of gloom" literally at a distance, in a reflection that not only conveys to him an image of what already has been shown to be an emblem for a lineage's slow destruction, but also suggests why everything happening in its place seems inverted, unnatural, yes, grim and ghostly:

> I have said that the sole effect of my somewhat childish experiment—that of looking down within the tarn—had been to deepen the first singular impression. There can be no doubt that the consciousness of the rapid increase of my superstition—for why should I not so term it?—served mainly to accelerate the increase itself. . . . I had so worked upon my imagination as really to believe that about the whole mansion and domain there hung an atmosphere peculiar to themselves and their immediate vicinity—an atmosphere which had no affinity

with the air of heaven, but which had reeked up from the decayed trees, and the gray wall, and the silent tarn—a pestilent and mystic vapor, dull, sluggish, faintly discernible, and leaden-hued.

Poe's story is this fog and vapor.

Poe's story is this fog and vapor, and the narrator encounters the same strange air when he is led into the studio where his old friend is waiting: "I felt that I breathed an atmosphere of sorrow. An air of stern, deep, and irredeemable gloom hung over and pervaded all." The impression is further strengthened when Roderick, "through broken and equivocal hints," describes the uncanny fear in whose clutches he seems restrained:

> He was enchained by certain superstitious impressions in regard . . . to an influence which some peculiarities in the mere form and substance of his family mansion had, by dint of long sufferance, he said, obtained over his spirit—an effect which the *physique* of the gray walls and turrets, and of the dim tarn into which they all looked down, had, at length, brought about upon the *morale* of his existence.

More need not be said about the exchange of attributes that is taking place in Poe's account between exterior and interior realms, between the decrepitude of matter and the despondency of spirit. The *house* is an image of the *family*: the gloom that holds Usher in its torpid power is the same that seems to breathe in the building's walls, turning its inhabitants into shells of former selves, vessels containing gray air and despair.

The word to underline in the passage quoted, then, using that thin mobile silhouette cast by the diminishing implement we still hold in our hand, is neither "form" nor "substance," but "influence," an imp of a notion that in this context must be taken figuratively as well as literally, as the gloom it embodies is distinguished by an ability, so disquietingly shapeless, to trail in and out of a person's thoughts, like Lazarus defying the laws of nature. It lacks form as well as content; is similar only to fog or vapor; and reminiscent of the springy – » – of repetition, it is capable of moving from one place to another, then mercurially skipping one before it eventually recurs at – » – further down.

Only matter as gray as stone seems able to prevent this uncanny commotion from strengthening its hazy dominion, yet it is of course precisely in this way that the atmosphere of Poe's plot thickens. In the world gleaming through its latticework, as if in the deep, oozy water of the tarn, dumb and seemingly dead substance may also be animated. After the lord of the castle has recited the ballad about "The Haunted Palace," and the first signs of approaching ending appear like cards tucked away in a coat sleeve, the discussion turns toward a theory that Usher asserts with unusual and excited passion: "the sentience of vegetable things." His theory is considerably more intrepid than normal animistic opinion, however, since it does not limit its applicability to the organic realm outside the world of humans (plants, vegetables, trees), but also includes "the kingdom of inorganization" (stones, minerals, metals). This "belief," the author points out, "was connected . . . with the gray stones of the home of his forefathers"—as if the thesis provided an example of Roderick's theory—and with that we have arrived at the circumstance that makes the lord of the house of Usher a doomed man and Poe's account an uncanny text about the uncanny:

> The conditions of the sentience had been here, he imagined, fulfilled in the method of collocation of these stones—in the order of their arrangement, as well as in that of the many *fungi* which overspread them, and of the decayed trees which stood around—above all, in the long undisturbed endurance of this arrangement, and in its reduplication in the still waters of the tarn. Its evidence—the evidence of the sentience—was to be seen, he said (and I here startled as he spoke), in the gradual yet certain condensation of an atmosphere of their own about the waters and the walls. The result was discoverable, he added, in that silent yet importunate and terrible influence which for centuries had moulded the destinies of his family, and which made *him* what I now saw him—what he was.

Having difficulty breathing, Roderick's existence is under an almost ageless pressure, established it seems according to the principle of one stone on another . . . on an . . . other on . . . . Ultimately it is the stress and strain of this accumulated gloom that makes the house of Usher—castle *and* family—fall. The hardly noticeable crack the narrator had seen reflected in the tarn before he approached the mansion—that "barely perceptible fissure . . . extending from the roof of the building, in a zigzag direction, to the base"—runs toward the end fully visible from top to bottom:

> While I gazed, this fissure rapidly widened—there came a fierce breath of the whirlwind—the entire orb of the satellite burst at once upon my sight—my brain reeled as I saw the mighty walls rushing asunder—there was a long tumultuous shouting sound like the voice of a thousand waters—and the deep and dank tarn at my feet closed sullenly and silently over the fragments of the *"House of Usher."*

"The manner," we cited earlier, and suggested that the time ever more filled with destruction—this grayening—in which family and residence meet their ruin also could be used to read the story of the house of Usher. The relationship between mansion and lord of manor is repeated, we suspected and now would like to confirm, in the alliance between theme and presentation. For if scrutinized more closely, the final sentences too reveal the obscurely zigzagging signature of grayening fissures. Dashes write the ending apart in the same manner as the crack in the façade is gradually widened, causing the mansion to crash and crumble, deftly swishing like the death-sentencing Z of a comic-strip hero. How can we otherwise explain that Poe writes the *"House of Usher"* thus, in italics and within quotation marks, a specification that in this form cannot refer to the castle and the lineage only, but must include also his own text? An uncertainty similar to the one Roderick had evoked when he recited the ballad about "The Haunted Palace"—"I fancied that I perceived, and for the first time, a full consciousness on the part of Usher of the tottering of his lofty reason upon her throne"—now causes the narrative itself to tremble: syntax disintegrating, Poe's description collapses with mute, malleable force, waves of silence closing over its fragments. All is over.

The story of Usher's fall—this being the vanishing point we wanted to arrive at—thus does not avoid being influenced by the swellings of the ballad inserted with such uncomfortable care. Like the "suspended lute" to which the text's epigram initially refers, and which is said to resonate as soon as it is being touched, Poe's account seems unable to render the fall of the house of Usher without announcing its own pending destruction. In the collapse that follows, the row of dashes mark graphic cracks—or strings—in which the grayening of the text finds its densest expression. Both precondition and result, cause and effect, this crumbling tremor can be neither maintained nor ignored. Suspended, it forces the construction to collapse "through its mere matter."

The most unpleasant conclusion, however, still remains to be drawn. For if Roderick's heart is a *luth suspendu*, set in motion as soon as it is touched, it can only be our reading of Poe's text that tears it apart. In the devastating economy established by the narrative, through a "doubling" to which it refers itself, it is reserved for reading to set in motion heart, chambers, and emotions. Rendering the fall of the house of Usher, the text seems agitated the same way Roderick's recitation of "The Haunted Palace" had disturbed the fragile order of his brain and heart. The final sentences of Poe's story may remain complete—just as the mansion's stones, which keep both weight and form despite their disintegration—yet they glide apart in a manner possible to observe only in the act that made the process appear and unravel.

In Poe, we may thus conclude, reading ultimately amounts to a reading-apart. To assimilate his text is to take in the rupture entailed in the inaudible dashes, registering the phonic fissures they signal like the lean strings of a lute. They mark a disintegration all the more uncanny as it is explicitly compared to "the gradual yet certain condensation of an atmosphere of their own," thus confirming Roderick's thesis that matter as dead and rigid as letters and signs can become animated—"a pestilent and mystic vapor, dull, sluggish, faintly discernible, and leaden-hued."

The uncanny in Poe's account of the house of Usher is that its text contains the vapor that this vapor is.

A grainy granitic gray . . . At the end of Poe's story, no stone is left upon stone; everything falls and falls apart. Perhaps we may consider this the inverse of Stein's rosary—*A stone is a stone is a stone*—a formula whose character does not stress a more encompassing, pliable and elastic identity hidden behind the apparent multiplicity of objects in the world, but rather the collapse of everything into particulars, fibrous and strident, like a cloud brimming with particles, a fog thick as cream, a smooth sheet of vapor sprinkled with grainy hail.

In Stein's *A rose is a rose is a rose* the flower must be so red that it ultimately turns blue . . . blue with longing and blue with desire's blushing plight and delight . . . blue and trembling, and blue and moist, caressing like honey and as warm as the tea in which it is dissolved . . . blue like throats surpressing their wailing, blue like melting mouths meeting, and blue like lips forming syllables in softly swollen, sensually swelling curves . . . *Eros is eros is eros* . . . not neglecting the many-headed virility thronging in its wagging stem . . . *Arrows is arrows is arrows* . . . as if only a plural noun joined to a singular verb could convey this rouse of a sentence . . . Amor throbbingly redfaced with blueish bow and abundant blue arrows . . . wagging, dangerously wagging, and at every caress still more wagging, blue and wagging and filled with danger.

"Poetry is doing nothing but using losing refusing and pleasing and betraying and caressing nouns," Stein argued in a lecture entitled "Poetry and Grammar" given several years after *A rose is a rose is a rose* had become one of the standard illustrations of Steinian style:

> When I said.
> A rose is a rose is a rose is a rose.
> And then later made that into a ring I made poetry and what did I do I caressed completely caressed and addressed a noun.

For Stein, poetry has to do with words—glossaries—vocabulary. The contrast to prose, which like water is devoted to what flows and follows, and therefore tends toward the period and the paragraph, the adverb and the verb, like flaming fire, poetry is committed to life, that is to names and things, that is to nouns. Less action, more matter. Still, movement may be found also in poetry, because it "is concerned with using with abusing, with losing with wanting, with denying with avoiding with adoring with replacing the noun" . . . that enterprise so similar to turning pebbles languidly in the mouth, slick with saliva and clicking against the tongue, hitting the back of the teeth or resting between lips; stones rebounding on the surface of water, once, twice, three and four times, only to sink toward the bottom in a movement most akin to a spike being bent; stones flat like spatulas and stones rugged like the striking surface on a match box; stones heavy as heads on Monday mornings, stones unbribable as gatekeepers, and stones hard as stones and thus numb as stones. Like the beloved's name, the good noun leads to heightened desire every time it is mentioned, more resolutely, more irrefutably, but changes it does as little as the name of the person loved and beloved. "And so that is poetry really loving the name of anything and that is not prose."

Yet if the noun is like stone, numb like stone and hard like stone, a name like stone and the name Stone, it can never be depleted. It offers resistance in the same way a cloud does not let itself be caught by some wishful hand, extended in a hopeless bid for union, or the stone refuses to be opened, stern and unyielding, like a closed door, but is diffused merely into indolent heaps of vapor or rollicking gravel. One must assume therefore that blue's desire never could be heard in a sentence as gray as *A stone is a stone is a stone*, for here everything is ordered and defined by the principles of grammar: subject, predicate, and complement, about itself, in itself, and after itself, yet nothing changes, nor does anything mean something else. Perhaps an ear as piercing as our newly resharpened implement may hear *Tone is a tone is a tone*, or for that matter *Atone is atone is atone* . . . as if each tonality could fall victim to its own opposite . . . but that would be the same as to say *To atone is to atone is to atone*, and thus to apologize for the exception that confirms the rule.

We will have nothing of it. In *A stone is a stone is a stone*, everything is as it should be, crisp and stable, staunch and cool. A sentence set in stone. Like this one. In the case of stones, thus, what is important are not synonyms or similes glittering with precocious wantonness, vapors blue like deceitful tremor, but rather the repetition stubborn as the desire, craving and persevering, with which the beloved's name is beseeched. It would be as misleading, however, to characterize as poetic a sentence such as *A stone is a stone is a stone* as to call it prosaic. It does not rely on the verb's pliable sensuality though it is periodic, nor does it surround itself with an aura of sonorous sweetness though it persistently caresses and addresses a noun. No. It is as prosaic as only poetry can be, and as poetic as prose still is. It is grammatical.

Let us further consider the difference, however, for it might suggest yet another way in which blue differs from gray—at any rate when we talk about "blue" and "gray," and thus deal in language. Both colors are concerned with duration, a remnant or recollection of things past, but if blue reveals a memory identical to a longing sufficiently intense to make the absence of its object as blue as the gorge of a sky—and to lose oneself in this abyss is the craving of every longing—gray represents rather the feeling *that* something has been forgotten, with nothing replacing it in its absence. At most there is a bit of blue sky babbling, as it were (and once was noted), through the troughs of torn clouds, but it soon vanishes again in an undulation of matte and bored movement. If blue memories thus let an individual be taken by surprise by the past, feeling their sticky fullness as if they were sugar candy between finger tips, gray memories do not permit recall, true or other. They are rather like pockets with holes in a pair of pants worn again after a long interval. Hands get lost.

Blue memories range from the sharpness of ultraviolet remembrance to the azure abundance of well-lived, if sad-tainted, memoirs (*sorrows is sorrows is sorrows*); it is a satiation in which time is caught and discolors, like caramels in the clenched fist of a child. Gray memories, by contrast, are heaps of vacuum and dust, a hunger feeding on itself, off itself, and thus able, gnawingly, only to increase. At most, a gray mouth would exclaim "Now, what was it . . . ?," but, well, never "O, it was . . . " or some similarly velvety variety of randomness and recollection. In the case of blue, absence is full and thriving, while here it remains as empty as a cenotaph.

Instead of an intense flame releasing life's rapture and bounty, gushing delight, there is only vapor containing but dearth and missed connections.

Yet both blue and gray have a tendency to withdraw . . . to disappear quietly when approached quickly . . . like noon-time shadows . . . which is not the case with yellow, for example, a color that both Goethe and Kandinsky held to be expanding in the way the sun drills its light into a silken eye filled with buoyancy (a whirling auger against which our gaze is powerless since all sight depends on light). But in blue, a person either gets lost because its dimness is so close and its attraction so great that every fall is sweet as a stroke, or because its brightness is so vast, its chill so open, that each breath expresses unconstrained freedom. To get lost here is to locate a deeper solidarity, another community, an absorption so fundamental that it may confirm an identity even behind a pronoun as hopelessly accidental as "I."

To be sure, we also get lost in the gray, but here everything remains uncertain—cloudy weather, cloudy memories, and often simply clouds; memories that appear, mellow fields, frosty mist, and still other clouds above darker fields. But wherefrom, and how? As fog or dusk will make any distance shrink without diminishing it in the least, like a long distance phone call, gray provides the kind of uncertainty accompanied by the feeling that something invisible is close by, yet it remains absent no matter how near it hovers. An umbrian companion. Or the inside of a wind. For in the gray we also lose ourselves, oblivious of direction, no longer retaining any hold on life. Yet nothing is offered into which we might immerse ourselves, no embrace as secure as that of the mother's blue bosom or the warmly lined inside of a winter coat, pulled out again from the closet. It is like being the shadow cast by nobody. And therefore uncanny. And therefore uncanny, and therefore vapor.

These assumptions would at most be theoretical, however, if we were not able to develop them and demonstrate that it is possible to read the difference between blue and gray. For indeed, it can be done. *Bl*, for instance, is the fullness of that rounded, slightly eroticized protuberance in *blue*, softly pouting with thick tongue and expanded cheeks, the lips' delightful expectation, indecent only when we do not dare admit our blue thoughts (and thus forbidden, like blue apples). Bubbling balloons slowly swelling like the little bump, no, lump, between *l* and *b* in *labia*. And do we not already hear how words are filling with desire? like the rough bulge on the bicycle tire that only awaits a jolt a trifle harder than usual, the edge of the sidewalk or a badly placed sewer grate, before it suddenly surrenders with first a wheezing, then a whistling sound (*ô vifs détours tout courus de caresses*), and the boy's legs stop pedaling as spontaneously as the pistons in his steam engine cease pumping if we remove the magical tablet . . . *gr*, in contrast, is gritty and scratching, like sandpaper, gravel arching its back under our rushing feet, or the narrow path cutting across the backyard where the bike now is placed, a roughness that rather resembles the cat's tongue on the back of the hand or the hair brush on that of the horse, or for that matter is brittlely antiquated in the way of a smell we happen upon in some long unused book in the library . . . Nothing to grasp, but still a corrosive past made perceptible.

Il fait gris, Clov says to Hamm, and adds: *Gris! GRRIS!* As tight and stiff as the movement of the tongue, a comb, or the pages of a book, this *gr* is fundamental in the manner of roots, rocks, and grammar. A certain steady regularity provides the same impression as the trembling spoon-bait that the shipwrecked—assuming he did not drown—cannot see but thinks he senses in fingers and spine as he weaves it up with his casting-rod, standing alone on the beach of a deserted island as elliptical in figure as a zero sign. The jerk with which this silvery copy of a fish pliably springs out of the water's depth is clearly distinct from the sound of a puncture: in the latter case, the friction increases constantly until the tire with its priceless air no longer is able to resist, but goes flat with a naturalness we are tempted to deem longed-for, while in the former case, we are dealing with an ending that wraps itself around the beginning like a spool of yarn tightly wound around its bobbin—soft, silent, exhausted. Both form and content, or rather: content because form.

It would probably be possible to make glossaries according to this difference. We have already mentioned the *labia*, but also *libido* and *lubricant, bless, blush,* and *blaze* are words as seductively alluring as polished shoes, or *siblings, bloom, bliss,* and *sable*, to quote a rather more famous stretch of *bl*'s, whereas *grain, granite, grate, grave, ground,* and *grit* remind us more of the mote in an eye glazed with desire. If blue is the hue of flowers wet with moisture . . . *Light sob of breath Bloom sighted on the silent bluehued flowers* . . . gray is gravel crackling dryly, an exhalation of warm air and one of dust, the fullness of time and its deposit. So if blue is the hand along the fur of the cat already mentioned, gray must be the fingers against its nap—as if blue could be read only from left to right, whereas gray rises in the east and sets in the west. Two different cultures and two alphabets for longing.

Blue can be any flower, supposedly, but mainly the one far removed, while gray remains unmovable like the pebbles in Demosthenes's mouth. Which is to say that blue resonates with the flowering flow of saliva, spittle, or ink, blushing but attractive, clandestine yet abiding, whereas gray can only bespeak the pencil's narrow trail, at once blurry and crisp. And as imperturbable as stone. Blue is humming humidity—we hear it—while gray remains dry as tinder, despite certain oceans, fish, and the occasional dispensation of some lacrimose spasm.

Although animated by the same mumbling mouth, *blue* and *gray* have no letters in common. And while both include two vowels, the ones in the former are conspicuously pure in sound, whereas those in the latter seem muddled by the loamy sway of diphtongese. More to the point, it may be asked whether the *ue* of *blue* is not the deep and open contour mouthed when we say *You* to our beloved, hence is as circular as desire, and thus in effect an *o* masked though barely concealed, that rotund form lips so carefully acquire when they spell and respell *A noir, E blanc, I rouge, U vert, O bleu*, spherically shaped into a pouting cone that carefully rolls the letters, gleaming like glass pearls, into the ear's soft, accommodating lobe. *O, you . . . O, blue . . .* is that not the sound made by hands when they shelter the light of a candle? echoed by emptiness when loss becomes too heavy for its heart? emitted even by the bathtub when forced to let out its water? *O* is a hollow so full of absence, so rich in want, that its opulence turns sonorous in the manner possible only for the apostrophe of pure addressing.

What would gray sound like if it could be found in this resonant alphabet, all syllabic awe and wonder? Perhaps a never before perceived sound disentangled from a language not yet acquainted with teeth and tongue, lips and jaws, a parlance before or after all speech? A cry emitted from an unfinished mouth of clay, say, slithering like drivel or patter? Slooping staggering and stuttering . . . rattling like the spectral leaves of fall . . . a laughter without lungs . . . Golem's unfinished tongue, perhaps? Or rather a combination of vocal impurities, a diphthong like *oe* or *eu*, for example? But both *oe* and *eu* belong to the language of brilliance—*oe* as in the much-praised *oeuvre* of aesthetic refinement, that luminous **WORK** produced by letters as steady as scaffolding, or *eu* as in *euphony*, this work's beautiful concord, so full of harmonious syllables and delicately balanced diction, with verses vibrating as wind will caress a willow. Gray is hardly counted among these vowelizations; its bastard writing does not belong here. But where should we seek, then?

Perhaps we may permit imagination to concoct something as rare as a triphthong, a hybrid combination of three snaky vowels—as in *oie-oie*? *Ioe, you*? *Ieo*? Or is it quite simply *ai* . . . as in Achilles's suppressed anger or the sadness streaking the hyacinth's leaf with mellow melancholy? *Ai* as in aimlessness and pain? *Ai* as in the nomadism contained in all air? *Ai* as in the wailing of Ajax? *Ai* . . . yes, well,

ai,

grai,

gray . . . first that hard, raspy sound, then a rolling graze and soft sway as if thawing into the haze of a face . . . but no, wrong, we err, it is merely an opening and closing mouth, that grainy sound transmutated into a shape, which, sealed by tears, gasps for air, gives in and then again snaps for air, discombobulated surely, and listlessly imploring, but stuttering only managing to imitate the grim gorge of emptiness as it senses the end closing in. Like the drowner's last cry dry of help. An O soon without figure. Nothing confined in that other zero, life buoy-shaped but unhelping, into which we shall all slip—first with a yelp, then with a last chilling holler.

So gray, the word and the condition, the color and the act, is everything we cannot reach, but to the effects of which we may still testify. "Color emerges out of gray," Benjamin once stated in an early remark on aesthetics, "not gray out of color." We protect the old lamp with care in no way second to that of blue desire, now rubbing and scrubbing as if we expected the liberation of our own drift and drive, and in the lamp's stomach unshapeliness is softly mixed into shape. Presently a vibrating pillar of smoke rises like the pencil graphite in its wooden shaft, releasing a compressed cloud so many times larger than its container that it seems to defy comprehension. But what we witness is still only traces, those small sprinkles or wriggling insects contained in the balloon before it broke, now swarming in front of us in an unending stream of ripple movement, leaving a glimmer behind as dusky and ominous as a question mark. And as utterly unattainable as a reflection in the mirror.

When we go about sentences of this kind, moving the unchanging pebbles from left cheek to right cheek, playing with them on—under—at—around—the tongue, but then realize that they do not particularly like it, and therefore spit them out in the hand where they lie like shiny wet fish on the dock—remember Beckett's Molloy?—the same imperceptible and strange phenomenon happens: we cause something that could not be seen and continues to elude us, constantly changing yet always remaining the same. Gray and grayening, we turn into imps of vapor.

§ Three

And it continues to elude us. Like ice cubes, for example, first dryly clinking, then damply crackling, then clearly dying on us in the drink. Or take the snowflakes, all ginger and pale, whose crystalline rotations we try to pursue in our slow, amazed way, but which make short shrift by disappearing into the teeming crowd of a drift. Or a word even, slithery like a slip of soap, surely unwilling to emerge from our vacant lips even if we were to increase our hapless hankering with a hand hitherto unproductive, in the hope that the word will now come forth thanks to a thumb numbly massaging the index and middle finger. Seizing the moment, we even allow the tongue to produce a spongy, palatal sound, as if testing the efficacy of the dentures, but the lips, gulping, close with an affected expression of *Je ne sais quoi*.

What a sham. It is all to no avail. Gray will continue to elude us. For what are we thinking? O. No. The word is not hidden inside us, taut and tacit, ready to emerge like a rabbit from a magician's hat, tucked away in a fold of illusory nothingness. It has its own ways. We may rub our fingers and let tongue and teeth produce their crazed concoction of noise and notion, but the word we are searching for will refuse to materialize. We can be sure of that. Only if we are sufficiently patient, neither dither too much nor desire too little, may it conceivably at times very well perhaps finally eventually maybe at long last arrive. But it is not likely to do so in the manner of a lost son, or some foreign friend, or the old lover, who all return with an air of displaced fervor as if trying to need us as much we want them. None of that. Not here. If at all, the word is likely to emerge more in the manner of Lazarus, dressed in ambivalence and mellow misgiving. Reluctantly it will peer through the void still stabbing that hole in our sentence, with sensitive eyes unused to the rim of light, irresolutely poised on the threshold between oblivion and blending-in.

Gray is, we have attempted to argue thus far, when nothing is . . . but . . . what *is* that? Is it the shape facts acquire when they fuse with forgetting? the look faces assume when nobody is watching, so similar to the trees in Bishop Berkeley's forest without God? Or is gray like the mirror in a hotel room (first floor), not giving us our identity, but granting us what is greater, anonymity? And by the way, now that we are here, what do we see there, swimming in that thin flat pool of foil and commotion? Perhaps a dotard who, shunning life and people, is about to come to an end the way a tape runs out? with a face made of hardened smoke and a batch of wrinkles of put-on wisdom? merging with nullity as if it had been scratched forth like the number on a losing lotto ticket? Perhaps he—for it does seem to be a he—it is a male—even sports glasses? or are those merely a pair of empty eye-sockets, big as a giant's thumb prints, facial indentations whose sides are pressed against the nose as if held together by a clothespin? Or is it rather a sagging figure of eight, slung across the vault of the nose like saddle satchels across the back of a horse? And what about that nose . . . quite prominent, is it not? Arched like the glossy shell of some rare, oblong insect entrenched in a face like a regular nightmare. Yes. Well. What? The lips? Then there are the lips, of course, full as only lips can be. No need for metaphors there. And. What about hair? Do we see any? There is that scratch of hexagonal white on the forehead, quite noticeable it is, too, like a patch of erratic chalk relocated from a blackboard . . . but hair? Hard to see; harder to say. The figure has barely had the time to disentangle itself from the background, it seems; the contours are still uncertain, the shape too indistinct.

Yet there are parts of clarity, obvious stretches of distinction. The right shoulder, for example, traces an edge of certainty on which that surrounding, unfathomably hovering void seems tilted. Like a block of frozen thunder. But no wobbly lines, really. Or take the chin and throat. Both support the centrality of the mouth in this picture, portrait, effigy—whatever it is. We did not mention that, did we? Well, the mouth *is* the center here. No doubt about that. What with the obtuse angle and all. Like a flaw becoming flower. So . . . so the scene we are privy to, whatever else it is about, it must be about seeing speech, or observing a mouth.

Yes . . . OK . . . but . . . you know . . . maybe the figure is receding rather, first veering slightly out of focus, then out of view, growing fainter as our lense turns foggy, retreating like steps down a staircase? Perhaps this is all about silence instead, that sullen, sulphurous afterglow of speech? And who is the person anyway, so defiantly off-handed, conjured forth by both *lapsus* and *lingua*? With the looks of, we must admit, a piece of furniture? Has he just arrived from the country, still confused as he sits down in front of his facsimile on this his first visit to the city? No, that would not do. Such a scene seems unlikely. Not here. There is no . . . well . . . the setting must be infused with more tension . . . yes, to begin with, more tension and cunning might . . . yet it should not display a single trace of suspense. Then agitation has to be added, but neutrality must prevail. And like wisps of mist and forgetting, the picture has to remain both distinct and diverting. All is uncertain in it, except the outcome. So, are we instead facing a prisoner sentenced to death? There is a thought. Perhaps it is that solitary convict with his back to the cell door, facing the thick gray wall through which our interdimensional gaze may nonetheless peer, as if equipped with a vision able to filter through even the densest flurry of granitic atoms, a turmoil of tough particles and relentless void? Or are we merely confronted with some old hand well acquainted with the wasting of time? That cardboard con man? Furtively causing fancies to loiter like fragments of a melody may linger in our mind long before we notice it? And who every time he returns to the anonymous room where this scene is laid out in front of him behaves as if he had never been there before?

Nonsense. Whichever way, the shoulders are broad and powdered with frail white dust, as if light had settled into a thin pattern of granular precision. And the head's straight posture, slightly bent back as it is . . . cheek protruding but forehead reclining, almost vanishing . . . yes, vanishing, like a flat stone slowly disappearing into a thick, gooey mass . . . well, such posture seems to suggest a certain confidence vis-à-vis whoever is the observer. "Resilience" is a word that may come to mind. But, oh, the overwhelming space of flatness and nullity that surrounds the figure is vastly more impressive than this hodge-podge of fog and profile for which our imagination is responsible. It is like a nebulous haze slabbed and polished into a slim plane; only wafts of white sediments are still making it fuzzy in certain areas. Come to think of it, the picture reminds us of a chalk-clouded blackboard, so we may even call it a "grayboard," following Timofey Pnin's fitting lead (no need to be coy about it, we have been saving his coinage for a moment like this). The odd thing, though, is that the figure hovers precisely at the level of the image's surface, as if it were a thin membrane extended inside a depthless foil or the suspended silhouette of a zero sign slightly shaken, then stirred out of shape. For there is no third dimension here, we would like to remark, yet plenty of volume and density. A woozy naught in a slow sea of haze and cessation. What deathless precision.

Areas of this kind of gray are usually to be found somewhere in the umber abode of a well-constructed story, in the anonymous middle of a chapter, in the rented room of a paragraph—in the deft indistinction that defines every carefully crafted sentence, in which syntax is a question as much of shade as of shape. Yet such places cannot be visited, even less may we pace their length or trace the distance from imaginary floor to chimerical ceiling, their inventories cannot be investigated, and the furniture they contain does not allow us to settle in like an old friend amidst pillows and ongoing parlance. At best we come upon them and get lost.

Dust,
vapor,
dust.

There. Or here. For they are zones with the sensuousness of an empty pocket. Receding, always receding. Vain orbs akin to the last gasps emitted from that mouth. Or the quizzical pupils of fish as the drowner sinks vertically into obliteration, a declawed asterisk, etherially spinning, in search of its final footnote.

It is in this direction, at any rate, that we find the heart of gray literature, or so we are beginning to suspect, like a cavity within a vacuum (a reference we regret has gotten lost), and from where we are, slightly above and across, we may discern a voice at times speaking from it as neutrally as the arid monody of a mute. Lazarus, for example, Mr. Absence himself, must have rested in such an anonymous space, like the dry spot under a wet stone. (Some suspended animation.) Just a pale vessel of rusty remembrance, adrift in desuetude, lucklessly forced to coordinate his steady thickening into consciousness with the spacing of indispensable vacancy. All because of some conjuror's need to impress. For what Lazarus had become, this frail pattern cast by joined jolts of missed heartbeats, could not be ignored or eradicated, however much he were brought to breathe again among those breathing. Traces of lead-hued vacuity always linger in any stab at second-degree existence. A memorable figure of . . . —forgetting, shall we call it?

This, at any rate, is the sort of nullity we have in mind. A living absence amidst the paltry props arranged by fate. It does not amount to mere avoidance and abstraction, but displays a certain keen distinction and that odd, somewhat dingy sort of delectability usually reserved for drop-outs. Yet to perceive such concoction of gray rootlessness and vibration as it wobbles through our present and living world with the tottery touch of cardboard is, of course, not an easy matter. For instance, it is not particularly noteworthy, or mellifluous, or variegated in the manner of certain people's memories of a private drawing lesson during a long lost childhood—

Now the colored pencils in action. The green one, by a mere whirl of the wrist, could be made to produce a ruffled tree, or the eddy left by a submerged crocodile. The blue one drew a simple line across the page—and the horizon of all seas was there. A nondescript blunt one kept getting into one's way. The brown one was always broken, and so was the red, but sometimes, just after it had snapped, one could still make it serve by holding it so that the loose tip was propped, none too securely, by a jutting splinter. The little purple fellow, a special favorite of mine, had got worn down so short as to become scarcely manageable. The white one alone, that lanky albino among pencils, kept its original length, or at least did so until I discovered that, far from being a fraud leaving no mark on the page, it was the ideal implement since I could imagine whatever I wished while I scrawled.

—but quite clearly quite genuinely more insignificant, faintly reminiscent of an uncle from the old land, caught in a photo, who amidst abrasive, well-to-do relatives decorously attempts to hide his worn-out shoes by turning the toes inward, hands resting on shiny knees, hair flattened with fingers and saliva. Entirely unimportant. A liability, more likely. Yet there it is, that one thin carbony smudge on the picture: our implement with its supposedly awful power. All crummy yellow with metal-hued wrinkles and hair the color of a dirty carrot.

Unlike the blue memory, which encompasses seven waters with the lithe languor of ink, and thus the entire past as undeniably as the smooth, irreproachable horizon, gray memories only leave aching cavities, deposits of nullity at best saturated with the sensation of one's own eminent non-thingness. Like a twelfth step on a staircase of eleven, say, with the sudden thrill of panic that is bound to follow, that wild contraction of muscles while the foot sinks down toward the phantom of a step, covered internally with its own infinitely elastic, though utterly barren material. Infused with forgetting. Always appearing in the rear mirror of remembrance, gray recollection thus does not jerk closer with every new detail we may gather up for pensive treatment, however much we try to sink into its peculiar past, but only continues to distance itself, like lachrymal discharges dissolving into the big Nihil. It provides the form in which oblivion only survives.

But we already said that. More than once. So let us return instead to our original inquiry before that line of carbon we assume we are following ceases to be an argument to wield like a stick and instead rolls back on us like a coil of thermal paper. The question was, was it not, what gray is when it is nothing. So. Is it nil null naught? Zilch? Vain? Void? Is it? Well, yes. Sort of. Sort of like zero, it is. For consider the situation: a designation quite as unsuitable as a school girl's generous glory above the capital I, o does not belong because, simply, it is not. A figure for nothing, it acts as a placeholder marking vacancy in a symbolic system that otherwise would lack a word for lack. Could not gray, as nothing, be thus defined? That hollow traced by oblivion?

Thirteen hundred years ago, this elliptoid figure was plucked from one of the shelves in the Hindu number system, polished and hung around the neck of an Arabic traveler's camel. His name was not Mustapha or Abdul. Next, it went on a difficult journey through deserts as dry as the skin on which it was often written and over waters as bottomless as its own interior. Until it reached the Western frontier of the continent and was put in circulation within the Arabic Mediterranean culture with the slow ease of a snowmelt. Rome and Christian Europe did not understand the figure and therefore rejected it with customary ignorance. But admittedly, theological considerations, all shroud and solemnity, may also have played a role, at least in so far as they were based on principles borrowed from Greek philosophy, which could not conceive of creation *ex nihilo*. It was not until the fourteenth century, at any rate, when its mercantile importance dawned on capitalists in Northern Italy, that zero was introduced in Europe. For the tradesmen, artists, architects, and scientists of the Renaissance, a mobile and abstract arithmetic was the necessary prerequisite for economic and technological progress. Hence double bookkeeping and the incipient need to calculate future profits and losses soon saw to it that Hindu numerals entirely replaced Roman. The abacus was put aside, paper and pencil were honored, and graphic calculation replaced gestural computation. Objections were shamed into a corner and given hoods as pointed as the far corner of an isosceles triangle.

Yet this arithmetic revolution required that zero be written. In the Roman abacus the sign had been marked by an absence which was used, but never mentioned. Zero was not even given a symbol, in fact, but constituted merely the absence of a pebble or a piece of either wood or bone on one or several rows of the counting-board. With the introduction of Arabic mathematics—where o marked a fixed symbol in a given numerical sequence that existed regardless of physical embodiment—zero acquired both name and face... *nothing can to nothing fall, / Nor any place be empty quite*... demanding, literally, to represent nothing. Thus o came to be the site for a nullity that had none. A place holder as empty as its own hold on—well, nothing, obviously.

No need to mention then, as we shall nonetheless do, that zero must fill a double function. It stands for what mathematicians term the "null set," that is, the class of absences of some certain kind of objects, but it also marks the beginning of a process. On the one hand it is a cardinal number, on the other an ordinal. The end of a rope or the circle this forms when displayed on the floor. In both cases, however, zero is a number signifying the absence of numbers: it indicates the origin of an (empty) quantity or a point that excludes the possibility of precursors. Both container and mark, urn and stamp. Bath tub and float. The former figure cannot be perceived in any other way than as a circle, loop, or ring, whereas the latter can be imagined only as a score, a point, a wound. Ring and fingertip, as it were. Thus a catalogue of everything this double zero is not—the ultimate Null Set—should not only be without ending, like two loops braided together into the figure of eight, but it must also include everything that it is not, without letting itself be filled by it. It reflects the emptiness of infinity in the same manner as the frail *pince-nez* of Nabokov's myopic French teacher, Mademoiselle O, fatidically mirrored his blue and ever bluer childhood.

So zero is no puppet, proxy, or person—let alone some dog of air. It is neither a weak number, nor the point at which water freezes, nor the intersection of the ink-hued horizon and a pen borrowing its tint, just as little as a page as blank as a vacant stare is nothing. The person in front of this sheet shining with emptiness is not null, even if the sign on his door asks for mail marked Null to be delivered here. The absence of daylight in the room in which he sits is not nothing, the silence to which he is listening not non-existent, and its breaking certainly not not an act of substance. Zero is neither a bald head, nor the navel hiding in the fold of a belly. The gear shift in neutral is not zilch and a happy divorce does not mean that the marriage had been without both profit and loss. Zero is not the breathless mouth of a poor swimmer or the vain fumbling of a person seized by unrequited love. Nor does o constitute the latter's perpetually renewed apostrophe, as empty as the mouth of someone with too sweet a tooth, or the buoy thrown to the former when he, all fear and surprise, discovers that the water is deeper than at first assumed. Zero is not the island where the shipwrecked survived living on roots, berries, and a few fish, not the dinky raft on which he left this place of solitude, not the hole made by the poorly mounted mast that caused his craft to sink. Nor is it the equator where he was rescued by a boat commanded by a captain dressed in a navy shirt, the vessel further occupied by a woman with a child at her breast and two sailors in whose coats silver buttons shone like dry chilly ice. Zero is not God.

When Poe, in "X-ing a Paragrab," had John Smith, decamped in Nopolis, ejaculate, *Why, the fellow is all O!,* his assessment of Mr. Touch-and-go Bullet-head was not worth null and nothing. And although in some northern parts of the world students are said to "nullify" their new colleagues during the first few weeks of the fall semester, and electricians everywhere do the same, it is claimed, when they ground the wall socket, their activities are neither the same nor nothing. Zero is not what is not found under the bed of a child fearful of the dark, the indentations made by high heels on semi-soft rugs, or the teeth's unevenly folded imprint in an unfinished cheese sandwich. It is not the grainy aftermath of Krapp's last tape, the silence gradually emerging when the train leaves the station, or the tunnel under the river through which its squeeking procession of cargo and commotion passes while above it a raft without mast is sinking. Odysseus's homecoming to Ithaca does not signify zero, although his name begins with the letter with which it is often conflated, and although he called himself Nobody to avoid the Cyclop's gluttonous hunger. Zero is not its own final *o*, losing itself in concentric void. Neither is it the giant's single eye, nor the slippery hole after it has been put out, melting down the cheek like sluggish tears. Zero is not the candle burned down to the warm sludge in the middle of a holder or Ophelia's lap where Hamlet wanted to rest his head. And it surely is not the dark crater appearing when an oak is uprooted from its slope during violent autumnal storms, or the empty envelope opened by Mr. Null on an incongruous Sunday (not nil, not void). Least of all is it the loop performed by a trapeze artist courting deadly danger before his hands clasp those of his partner, not naught either.

Zero times zero does not constitute the number of circles in Dante's inferno, the buttons on an elevator panel, the rings that glasses may make, or flat bicycle tires, the retinal imprint of light bulbs when eyes are closed, nipples without baby mouths, or baby mouths without nipples. They are not the wiry spirals in a notebook, hollow cheeks, ice cube containers without water, or for that matter the word *without* in iterations without end. Neither are eggs, coins, or crowns null and naught, nor ears, testicles, nor solar eclipses. Zeros are not buttonholes.

The point—certainly not null—is obvious. A catalogue of everything zero is not remains inexhaustible, because even if we would succeed in writing down all the possibilities, listing each detail, every aspect, any item, which zero is not, ourselves included, the list itself would remain—also if we were to include it as the last article before the end. Which is to say that no matter how detailed the catalogue, and it must claim exhaustiveness, it cannot provide us with an empty quantity, and thus cannot be null. It falls outside itself like the rings left by a skittish stone skidding across shallow water. Zero is not zero is . . . not . . . zero is not . . . . Still, the number is clever as a car dealer in hiding this one true fact about itself, for if we formulate our understanding mathematically—writing, say, 0+0+0+ ... , or for that matter 0-0-0- ... —the result would nonetheless remain =0. In the manner of Russian replicants our null is hiding the zero that it is not under the generous hem of its copious skirt.

At most, we may thus infer, squinting askance, zero is its own division, all double and naught, without it however being able to ascertain such truth by straightening out and insinuating itself as the thin slash separating two voids. Like that sign signalling percentage. Or closed scissors, say. (But more indecent metaphors could easily be concocted here.) King Lear—*an O without figure, a nothing*—was not able to fathom such truly odd equation, which, as we know, cost him everything, including kingdom, wit, and sight. Toward the end of Shakespeare's play, this un-figure tries to appeal to Cordelia's heart by evoking a family fantasy as suspect as the metaphor we just chose to pass over: a "prison" where the two of them alone, like "God's spies," "shall sing like birds in a cage." Lear dreams of a place not to be found in any geography, alien to maps, missing in all topographies. A cell behind the heavy bars of things (I I I I I I). It is a site in want of a site, cloistered from tumultuous reality, inaccessible to the tentacles of power, spared the dismal decay of time. At this place of double removal, father and daughter may live in untouchable irreality. Hence: a gray zone, most akin to a spectral abode where things happen "comparatively," to use the term C. contrived for himself. In this involute space (yet another article on our list, this time the *o* housed in every void), Lear believes he will be able to live with Cordelia as secret agents and divine representatives—that is, as signs for signs. Finally, Shapesphere, as *Finnegans Wake* addressed him, has Lear understand the uncanny quality defining the "nothing" he has become. But too late; Lear is, in Krautspeak, *leer*.

Such *O without figure* must also be considered in its rhetorical aspect, however, not as a number, that is, but as a specimen of speech. For its arcane orb may well be both the hidden navel of some numerical pattern and the sonic halo formed by rotund lips willingly helped by nasal cavities and a tongue making a concave

imitation of the palatal sky above it, yet it exhibits form and shape merely in a manner of speaking. So . . . it looks like we, too, *modo figurativo*, may have arrived at a place where everything is "comparatively," that quaint site where a speaking being is being-so-to-speak. Yes, we seem to have returned to the mouth we never left. At long hollering last.

For Beckett's Molloy—a "black speck" "in the great pale stretch of sand"; apparently "in constant bladder discomfort," as Nabokov once noticed—this gray gorge is merely a cavity to fill with "sucking stones." The sixteen pebbles he finds by the sepulchral sea, tucking them into his four pockets like true *trouvailles*, provide a way to keep the organ of speech occupied in the absence of words. For his precursor, Demosthenes, training on an Aegean beach alive with solar whimsy, speaking with stones cluttering the mouth had served the purpose of making syllables agile, phrases nimble, the pitch of diction crisp and clipping. Streaming outward, becoming that "servant of thought" of which Plato spoke, rhetorically shaped speech was to be made/made to become a seamless fluid. By providing obstacles for articulation—no amusement without ache—the tongue would learn how to shape soap-bubbly bundles of meaning out of airy nothing, arranging them in floriferous patterns of surprising elasticity and that desired persuasiveness, trim and triggered. A few thousand years younger, struggling on a different beach, sullen Molloy is of another opinion. For him the mouth remains the cavern it really is, as empty as the zero sign, as pitiless as a pit. Still, refusing to remain virtual, obstreporous syllables may clot into existence, like wordlike worms of wad wriggling their way around a cavernous chaos. In contrast to Demosthenes's polished pebbles, Molloy's sucking stones serve to stuff this trough with mute, unflinching matter—to silence, finally, all that teeming claptrap. It is the void of endless voicing that Beckett, with typical low-key limpidity and spells of time and trouble later, will refer to in his last text, *Stirrings Still*:

> Such and much more such the hubbub in his mind so-called till nothing left from deep within but only ever fainter oh to end. No matter how no matter where. Time and grief and self so-called. Oh all to end.

If for Demosthenes the mouth presents the affable area of orality, the place where speech alone happens as it gives figure to thought and texture to time, for Molloy it remains an arcane indentation marked by noise and nonsense. A looped-tape extravaganza. By placing pebbles in his mouth, the former hopes to be able to shed the debilitating shackles of inarticulateness and acquire the skill to clothe the limbs of language in precious tints and taints, whereas the latter only wishes to live in its ramshackle absence. Aided by our battered Latin dictionary, we may excavate two designations in order to keep these types of mouth apart: *os* and *bucca*. With the first we would like to signal the locality where matter of various kinds goes in and out, but above else that strange substance of air-turned-syllabic, whereas we shall set the second aside to refer to the site of the mouth's doings when it does not do language—the abode accommodating all that breathing, coughing, hemming, hacking, smacking, and sucking. Like a form without content, or rather, come to think of it, like an O without figure.

A way of happening, then,

a mouth.

Now let us try to steady this underdeveloped distinction by defining the particularity of Molloy's kind of embouchement as containing a certain sort of grain, absent in our *os*'s strainless stringing of sound into sense. For with this we may arrive at a new element and thus to finger number three—the one with the ring, that is, with which we will signal renewed commitment to our gray pursuit. As we perceive it, borrowing a few lines of thought from an essay on voices, grain is that which is body in speaking. It cannot be reduced to a distribution of morphemes, we would thus wish to suggest (with Roland Barthes, who wrote the text), or of words, or of phrases, and least of all to the purveying of fine and fettled patterns of meaning. Yet grain is always to be found in the manner in which action turns into act, in that microchasmic passage between gesture and gist. Take the clearing of the throat during some semi-forced confession, for example, when laryngeal hesitation clings to the contour of ensuing statements, or the draft of silence in the library when each whisper is made so wistfully palpable, or the pulse's beating in a verb, the shrill sheen of shock in a cry of surprise. Without these traces of bodiliness our ears would not remember, limbs not jerk, thoughts not recoil, for there would be no intriguing patch of fibrous friction just this side of fancy.

From which follows—albeit at some remove—that to speak without grain is fatal. A statement, report, or description may be perfect in form, executed according to all the rules of language and shaped with both care and knowing, but without grain it is as uninteresting as a day without mail. To persist with a phrase or paragraph until it has reached its particular perfection—with the same attentiveness, say, that a mother watches the milk to prevent it from boiling over—is certainly an honorable doing, worthy of our bluest praise, but without some blemish or stain, thus without finitude, and therefore perfect, even such patient labor would be nugatory. Merely a well-crafted sentence, a precious phrase, a blue sanctuary in which nothing is alive. The polished shot at a pointless gloss. Beauteous but boring.

Rigor, sharpness, brilliance . . . respect for the rules of elocution and overall oral savvy: technical know-how can *flatten* language to perfection. Grain, in contrast, provides it with that necessary tremble, that throaty throb calling for an impossible touch, which makes it stick and stay steady in mind. A blurry but dutiful beat. Even if this means, as indeed it must, that this or that amount of language will remain a shade rough or gauche in aspect, with the finish at best of an unshaven face, grain alone is grace. And although we immediately recognize it, readily spotting its flawful palpitation in any slick slew of sentences, like a wiry protrusion in an otherwise lean context, it remains impossible to determine exactly the cause from which is derived the peculiar impression that grain never fails to give. For even when we permit an imaginary audial hand to glide smoothly across the unkempt surface of what has been said, each quiver registered as if on a private Richter scale, or when the wife slides hers over the cheek of the abovementioned face, neither we nor she would be able to tell precisely what vouches for its strange allure. No, grain cannot be learned or taught. It does not invite to pedagogical proclivities.

A formal letter, for instance, just to concoct a quick example, ought to be written with proper measure of both precision and reserve. For this purpose a metal black diction seems most appropriate, we would imagine, one whose point has the matte gloss of an olive or at least the same sinuously menacing character as the cord of a modern shaver. A father's letter to the lost son living on foreign soil, on the other hand, should be composed in brown-hued prose with streaks of grainy violet to allow compassion and controlled grief to speak out of each line, whereas the devotion in a love letter can breathe only in arrays of red impetuosity: the ruby of passion, for example, as deep as that of a tomato, open and defenseless like a wound, or the currant-colored flame with claps of thunder contained like spells of anxiety barely kept in check, or a much-too-sharp tone of crimson inscribed with edgy reproaches like a margin with the comments of a teacher, or that rusty hue dipping lightly but deftly into decline, from which speaks an enthusiasm ready to dry into habit. Letters to friends can be written only in shades of green (copious and verdant like the leaves of mid-summer; clear and glossy as dish detergent; tough and cropped like golf lawns), advertisement should be composed in pale yellow tongues, and congratulations or compliments function best in a style somewhere between the shiny peel of an orange and the manila envelopes obtainable in pudgy kiosks in several countries.

Without grain, however, this motley crew of missives would merely be a pro forma tabulation of epistolary tactics. None of the messages would need to be kept, none worthy of remembrance. Still we are loathe to tell what finally makes the bureaucrat listen or the son's chest turn heavy with the weight of kin, the lover sense the pulse pound plushly in his wrists (and then, after the obligatory second read, feel the beating recur beatifically in the groin, too), the friend's face crack into the munificent disarrangement of a smile, the casual offer be both shelved and remembered, or gifts appreciated with ardor agog—because there it is, that *quelque chose de grisant* on which it seems so difficult to put our third finger. It is not the words themselves that cause it, but rather a shade of dry shudder, a thin abrasion breathing within their enclosures or between their frames, separating the phrases in which the words are embedded from the teeming confusion surrounding them like so many clouds of clustered cuddling. A quiver and a crack. A fissure. That certain "it."

If we were to pour these letters through a filter, issuing their lush thick light lax sticky spraying fluid into a cone-shaped fold hastily fabricated for the occasion, hoping to distill some distinction similar say to the downy sediment at the bottom of the lab assistant's test-tube (or in the pockets of her work coat), only periods, commas, hyphens, and other features of diction would remain, however.

Dust,

vapor,

dust.

Again.

So it must be grain, this rickety nothing, that makes the difference. As insignificant as punctuation marks, it tacitly provides forms of statement, frames for phrases, patterns of plot. And these graphite thickenings for that matter, which we tend not to notice, they, too, are such beings without being. Try to speak them alive. Like *Père Joseph*, they conceal themselves in the mute hollow of their own shadow. Yet every word, to be sure, was born with such a silent pang of punctuation, issuing with a grim electric throb from relentless Cadmian obscurity.

The only image we are able to concoct in order to describe this gray area is rather humdrum, we must confess, and as such barely feasible to be admitted as a plausible piece of evidence. But we imagine an apartment in which for several decades the floors have not squeaked from scattered crunches of footfall, the walls not absorbed the incandescent thrills of illicit breath, because of— let us say—a domestic feud or some dispute over an inheritance, or simply because the family who used to occupy it died out, except for an old bachelor who worked at a miner's homestead far away and then, during one of his wanderings, fell from a cliff up country, which forced him to change trade and stick to the level expanses of the ocean, where, however, he shipwrecked not much later, unused to the agile mounts and valleys of the aquiline temper, and was stranded on a deserted island for thirteen years or so before he finally succeeded in building a raft on which he took off—with unknown outcome for most (but, alas, not for us). Dust covers this place with its thick coat of decay: the many chairs, the wardrobe with the lead-veined mirrors set in its gangly doors, the night stand with its spider-like legs, the old desk as steady as an ox's breast, the sleeping bunk with springs gaily sprung, the book case and its books, all items in adipose oak and stout mahogany. Covered in dust. Everywhere. In recesses seemingly impossible to reach, in nooks and crannies, along narrow paths and across thin panels, dust treks its spurious trails of presence. There it is, hiding under the bed or insinuating itself into its spread. Or over there, either fluffed into feathered balls blown silently into far-away corners or heaped up to be scattered in the granular expanse of a rug. Or right here, gathered into shapes of downy duplicity so cunningly connived it even now is hard to see it abandoned on chair shoulders, tabletops, lamp hoods. Vertical exhalations of mealy powder have been brushed against the walls, this mirror, that door, even smeared onto these windows and those curtains. There is dust reminiscent of pollen panted amply on tilted surfaces and there is dust that recalls the damp mold forgotten things may release so absent-mindedly into the world. Vast waves cover the vistas of a floor and miniscule, derelict wreaths surround a chair leg or a bulbous curve. Fabulous, frivolous dust in all ware and everywhere . . . always different yet indifferently the same.

It strikes us that such must be time's body. For it provides skin for every edge and exterior, shape for all extremities, contour for every convex and concave. Nothing is grim but everything is gray. And in this lies the obscurely twisted attraction that pulls us into the picture. Because scrutinized more attentively, the objects in this forgotten place do not possess shape; rather it seems to be the dust that provides them with texture, emphasizing this flatness, creating that volume. As if time could only appear when thus marked, turned into an aspect of space. In due course, the furniture will disappear, so much is certain, not through irregular seizure or regular decay, but simply because it will dissolve into the wide dispersion out of which it once was born. Dust shall sink into the objects and slowly change their configuration into atoms of mere ash and silly nothingness, vast chalky clouds full of abandon and dispersal. Gray, grayer, and finally so gray that not even indistinction may be discerned. Time, we wish to propose therefore, when not measured, is nothing. A missed heartbeat.

In the same way that dust conveys edge and contour to the emptiness just described, punctuation marks provide shape and stay to language. They give birth to sentences, in a manner of speaking, gently arranging the limbs, shaping their body; in the process they may even convey rhythm and reason. For there is, we are inclined to believe, some construal before construction, a certain conception before creation, and this is the gray recalcitrance out of which everything seems to emerge, and into which we all will disappear. Yet in themselves, these traces of graphite constitute but scattered reminders of the same anonymous chasm out of which words once were culled and to which they are bound to return. For each punctuation mark also incarnates finitude. It is merely the fleeting token in some endgame played by an implement used to test the tics and tissues of its shortspun life.

Only few of these fibs of finitude found favor with Stein. The question mark, for instance (finally we may shed that shadowy fleece of an allusion), was "the first and the most the completely most uninteresting" sign in what she termed *one's writing*, a superfluous graphic loop that at most was thought useful as owner's mark on sheep or other livestock, since its nature was already implied in the form of the sentence. To end with such twisted sign was clearly as redundant as giving thanks for the lamb chops prepared by oneself. It was also not very respectful of a sentence's ability to speak for itself. The same held true for the exclamation mark and assorted inventions used to signal citation, according to Stein, even including those twinkling guillemets so similar to the corner of eyes when tears are rubbed away with rough abandon. Hearing the shape of the sentence, listening to a rising pitch or a falling cadence, discerning the shadow cast by imported speech, we should be able to conclude both what is said and how it is intended to mean. No need for decor.

The situation is slightly different, however, as Stein conceded, in the case of periods, commas, colons, and semicolons. Whereas the signs used for questions and exclamations merely confirm the structure of the sentence they close, leaving the phrase the way the palm does a door handle, a period, comma, or colon mete out the syntactic length (hence the life) of what is said, and thus belong more properly to the motion produced by it. No mere garnish, then, but tacit signs signaling the pace with which a thought is bent, so to speak, or the place where an impression is twisted and turned about, the space an attribution will need to unfold. These markers of punctuation also determine whether a sentence will end the moment our supply of air dwindles to a thin bolt of black void or whether it ought to include an otherwise empty dig—a pause, a caesura—where we may catch our breath in order to continue the journey of saying with renewed vigor and inspired perseverance toward an ending that is still not clearly visible, but whose imminent arrival nonetheless is presaged by certain signs scattered like dark-hued debris along our way, as if these cut-off nails, spurs, or whatever they are were mortgages on an ending, silent milestones moving into, then past our attention on this trek toward an end that is still bound to occur, yes, we know it, but now we also feel it, almost see it, that stone-solid, sudden stop. (. . . *"death," Sleptsov said softly, as if concluding a long sentence.*)

"Inevitably no matter how completely I had to have writing go on, physically one had to again and again stop sometime," Stein wrote in one place, "and if one had to again and again stop some time then periods had to exist." Which consequently suggests that a period, like other forms of punctuation, belongs to the body of language, and is conditioned by breath. It does not merely offer some rotund jar with black gold at the end of a sentence glistening in the spectral fluorescence of a haphazardly curved rainbow, but also has a semi-life, a quasi-spirit of its own, and may appear whenever it wishes. "Stopping sometime did not really keep one from going on," Stein continued, "it was nothing that interfered, it was only something that happened." Periods do not intervene, then, but occur rather, as capricious as death, and as necessary as the signature at the bottom of the receipt with which the prisoner hands over his belongings. In contrast to commas and colons, these wretches of writ, they do their own thing:

> Periods have a life of their own a necessity of their own a feeling of their own a time of their own. And that feeling that life that necessity that time can express itself in an infinite variety that is the reason I have always remained true to periods so much so that as I say recently I have felt that one could need them more than one had ever needed them.

The period thus, whether stumbling block or stepping stone, empty as the eye after it has shed its tears or pregnant with stiff silence like a frozen pupil, is always definitive... yes, even more final than a last word. The comma, colon, and semicolon, on the other hand, depend on application and convention, and are thus reduced to serve more practical purposes: to urge on a saying, say, or to clarify the target of a statement, to join syntactical limbs into a gait with steady posture and even progress. All said and done, the period then appears, a somber fellow clad in unconditional black, first passing, then concluding the sentence. Ping. The distinguished thing.

Despite the dark, deafening glory of the period, there is one sign whose secondary, thus rib-like, character Stein seems especially taken to and prefers—the ornamental, but in no way decorative, genitive apostrophe:

> I can see and I do see that for many that for some the possessive case apostrophe has a gentle tender insinuation that makes it very difficult to definitely decide to do without it. One does do without it, I do, I most always do, but I cannot deny that from time to time I feel myself having regrets and from time to time I put it in to make the possessive case. I absolutely do not like it all alone when it is outside the word when the word is a plural, no then positively and definitely no, I do not like it and in leaving it out I feel no regret, there it is unnecessary and not ornamental but inside a word and its well perhaps, perhaps it does appeal by its weakness to your weakness. At least at any

rate from time to time I do find myself letting it alone if it has come in and sometimes it has come in. I cannot positively deny but that I do from time to time let it come in.

Nothing unusual, nothing surprising. Yet we would be hard pressed to find a more insinuating passage than this, although not a single indecency has been uttered that could soil its pleated surroundings. There has been neither a xxxx named, nor a xxxx called—nor a xxxx mentioned, for that matter, the activity to which xxxx and xxxx are said to succumb—these four-letter pollutants whose filthiness today merely consists in the way in which they still stain walls in subway stations, hoardings on construction sites, stalls in public toilets. For who, hand crossing heart, is shocked any longer by xxxx, xxxx, or xxxx, if not at most by the brutality with which these words shrink and shrivel from everything they intend to stand for?

In the sinuous stretch of speaking just cited, Stein does not lose a single word on things of this nature, nor is it clear to what extent we may read raciness into her phrases. Yet it is precisely this uncertainty, we would venture, that makes the passage teasing to our mind: it moves in insinuating ways, thus setting thoughts nimbly in motion. Let the apostrophe attached to plural words hang where it does, limp like a coat belt caught in the door of a car. If perchance it would wedge itself, excited, to the noun to which it, after all, can lay claim genitively; so be it; let it pass; it shall pass. Soon that cocky push of possessiveness will be punctured, we may rest assured, and air let loose, after which this crumbling hook of a genitive will serve only to provide us with the silhouette rendition of a deflated balloon. With the possessive case apostrophe within a word, however, the matter is different. Take Stein's mention of *one's writing*, for example. Quiveringly the tap points downward with shy, sly determination. A glistening tumescence similar to the one between *b* and *l*. A livid stalactite or tender little cone in a moist sheath of emptiness. Such is the ornament adored in Stein: a shiver suspended inside the well of a word. And despite the absence of singular genitives, this is a blue way to write about gray.

Returning to our decreasing line of inquiry, we wish to propose that grain consists of such virtually imperceptible necessities; and like tears and dust it is manifold. Thus it matters little how much blue time and bluer effort we may expend to make syllables sling together in amorously chosen words, permit sentences whether short or long to relate as lovers, or make paragraphs manage their emotional resources like a parent with many children. No matter how skillful the mouth may be in salivating syllables, without grain the effort will be as useless as a coin in a foreign currency. A sentence such as *l'ambre, le musc, le benjoin et l'encens*, for example, with which Baudelaire unfolded an oasis of clarity in the dense expansion of one of his better known poems, appears at first sight so distant from reality that, in comparison, the air in which it vibrates seems a manufactured miracle of solidity. Impossibly gleaming in blue, like a block of ice emitting streamlets of frosty fragrance in rueful heat. To be sure, the line contains suggestive reverberations from unreal provinces and exotic realities, tinged with an allure as soft as the inside of water, shimmering with the oily suppleness of lotioned skin, but the tinny coolness that the sentence offers, the grain it nonetheless reveals, is still there, amounting in this case to the strophe's rippling keys of shifting stresses . . . *l'ambre, le musc, le benjoin et l'encens* . . . scented vapor drawing the shady figure of vowels in a tinnitous cursive. Baudelaire provides the air necessary to breathe the poem with a pellicle as thin as the wispy paper that once sheathed illustrations in precious books. Those wavering words bring foreign flavor into our mouth.

Grain, then, is as light as this *peau de l'air*, a fleet of etherous accents which, when softly gathered on a sheet of paper, leaves a thin, vivid film of webby dust, reminiscent of shadows casting their nets of black lace across surfaces of sated water. This is not Mörike's famed snowflake, which having caused the bell to ring, melts away in lachrymous pensiveness, but rather ash scattered with wicked, filigree fineness. Smoke stiffening sound into sign. Wells of words well-wrought usually contain such quiet pendulums of stress thinly clanging in the syllabic interior of silence retained. Why, yes, for silence is an infinitely malleable material, not merely the removal of resonance but a phantomatic and pliable motion—like the cool silkiness of intricate bones, say, doing their bit of movement in a jaw or an elbow.

It is not surprising, then, that the singular genitive apostrophe's attractive slip of a slope is related, in our mind, to what Greek grammarians once termed "coronis," that clawlike, lilting little sign (') that marks the contraction of, according to one grammar, "the final vowel in a one- or two-syllabic word with the beginning vowel of the following word in order to avoid the meeting of two vowels." Such bending, which incidentally is the word's original meaning, identifies the sudden loss of a letter, like the swift disappearance of a sound in words spoken hast'ly. A short suspension and an emptiness marked, it is the spot where something went amiss. Or a cupped hand bending time into pending time. And similar to the navel, this quick claw is not part of the resonant body to which it belongs, but rather the missing clue. A void-made matter. Grain.

A mouth that speaks with grain thus must be gray. But always also semi-something else,
  not song but singing,
  not singing but sounding,
  not sounding but straining,
  not straining but groaning,
  not groaning but lamenting,
  not lamenting but wailing,
  not wailing but whining,
  not whining but whimpering.
  Whimpering, and hardly even that.
  Insignificant Josephine, the singer in a clan of mice whose members "on the whole do not care for music" and do not seem to understand it, is nonetheless the last gray voice before "the steadily faster dissolution of all bonds." "She has a love for music," Kafka writes, "and knows too how to transmit it; she is the only one; when she dies, music—who knows for how long—will vanish from our lives."

Despite this peerless position, the song Josephine produces is not particularly remarkable. If it really were, then

> her singing would have to give one an immediate and lasting feeling of being something out of the ordinary, a feeling that from her throat something is sounding which we have never heard before and which we are not even capable of hearing, something that Josephine alone and no one else can enable us to hear.

"But in my opinion that is just what does not happen," the narrator continues, because "I do not feel this and have never observed that others feel anything of the kind." Josephine's singing is devoid of what normally singles out song from the usual clutter of speech. Lacking timbre, volume, coloratura—the features we have learned to associate with voice made vast and wishful—it seems to consist merely of repeated, softly hummed *korones*: ' ' ' ' ' ' '.

Although Josephine does not really sing, then, but rather squeaks—perhaps "hardly rises above the level of our usual piping"—her mouth produces something unusual and exquisite, even alarming. A song without song. The piping that she brings forth during her performance in the auditorium "comes almost like a message from the whole people to each individual." What is speaking in this voice that hardly speaks? so seemingly dispossessed of what makes us listen, become captivated, be carried away? Even if Josephine's performance appears to contain the promise of something with unimagined importance for her and the future of her people, the audience remains noticeably indifferent:

> Josephine . . . can pipe as much as she will, or sing or whatever she likes to call it, that does not disturb us, that suits us, that we can well put up with; any music there may be in it is reduced to the least possible trace.

As good as zero and zilch, reduced to "the least possible trace." Trifle tunes. Bottom-of-the-barrel ditties. Still these moments of emptiness manage to capture the audience, inviting it to a blissfully sober inebriation, because Josephine's song—almost nothing—knows how to create space, room, range, thereby granting respite in the tumult of daily tasks. It offers no blue heights with the promise of expansive vistas, that much is certain, but gray, almost blank sockets of calm, similar in nature to the plosive pauses straying in the speech of a stammerer. Hardly more than a hole, hack, emptiness, yet still a voice cooling like wildest solace.

> She calls it pearl-like, we call it staccato; but at any rate here it is in its right place, as nowhere else, finding the moment wait for it as music scarcely ever does. Something of our poor brief childhood is in it, something of lost happiness that can never be found again, but also something of active daily life, of its small gaieties, unaccountable and yet springing up and not to be obliterated. And indeed this is all expressed not in full round tones but softly, in whispers, confidentially, sometimes a little hoarsely. Of course it is a kind of piping. Why not? Piping is our people's daily speech, only many a one pipes his whole life long and does not know it, where here piping is set free from the fetters of daily life thus setting us free for a little while.

Josephine's squeak is so insignificant that it is easily overlooked. It lacks the song's swinging lifts as well as the suspended mat that music may weave, this teeming matter of sonorous sways; it is more akin, in fact, to tones evaporating than to the vibrato teasingly hidden in the back of a tremulant voice. So her song must be closer to disappearance than to presence, belonging to a mouth as gray as funny-looking fumescent ash. Her song, that is, is at best the remembrance of song, the tune of loss. Thus, as we may guess, Josephine's road "must go downhill":

> The time will soon come when her last notes sound and die into silence. She is a small episode in the eternal history of our people, and the people will get over the loss of her. Not that it will be easy for us; how can our gatherings take place in utter silence? Still, were they not silent even when Josephine was present? Was her actual piping notably louder and more alive than the memory of it will be? Was it even in her lifetime more than a simple memory? Was it not rather because Josephine's singing was already past losing in this way that our people in their wisdom prized it so highly?

A familiar path by now.

When the old man disdainfully stares us in the eye, as in Anette von Droste-Hülshoff—

> then one sees the wrinkled face turn pale;
> bitter the gray mouth sounds, with hateful sneering

—it is a similar reminder, pale as a sheet, of the dispersion we have all been and shall again become. Like a letter in the mail: soon enough it will find us thanks to forwarding and despite fines. We shake the dust off our feet, protect ourselves with socks and thick-soled shoes, but it sneaks in while we gasp for air, begins to breathe among phrases, in and between words no longer simply ours. As inevitable as dust. And as shifting. Because a mouth that can die, thus is finite, and therefore must be a bearer of grain, can only be gray.

The following person might have been Josephine's brother if he had not been known as Gracchus, the Hunter. For a long time he worked as a miner in a forest where he often could be seen poking about among bushes and roots, but now we find him on a ship without rudder, roving across the polished sheets of seven oceans hunting for an eighth, fabulous water, resting on a wooden pallet, a dirty fringed silk cloth with a flowery pattern covering body and legs, "hair and beard, black tinged with gray, having grown together inextricably." This Gracchus lives in an empty "wooden cage," writes Kafka, "driven by a wind that blows in the undermost regions of death," but on waves belonging to a water beyond, "some earthly sea or other." A site without place, thus always in motion. Only doves announce his arrival.

Kafka's strange figure arrives in a town on a vessel that seems to be carried above water rather than floating on it. Three boys are playing dice by the wall and a little girl is filling her bucket at the fountain. The accompanying doves, which earlier swarmed around the belfry, have now settled in front of the yellow house to which Gracchus—not without difficulty—is carried on his bier. Fluttering noisily, they peck at the window pane, depositing their silvery treasures. Presently the bearers are putting down their burden in "a cool spacious room looking toward the back" on the first? second? floor; then they try to light several candles at the head of the bier. "Yet these did not give light, but only disturbed the shadows which had been immobile till then, making them flicker over the walls." Only few people venture to this place, and only rarely.

From the other side of the yard a stranger is observing the beginning of this scene, shakes his head in disbelief, as if he did not trust what his eyes were witnessing, before quickly proceeding toward the door. But wait. Stop this scene for an instant; retain that breath in the throat. The stranger seems suddenly to have frozen, as if he had just encountered a ghost. Remarkable. What could it mean? Probably it is just a chance incident, but let us at least take note of it before we flip on the speed again. Tuck it into the pocket. So. There. Now we may continue. Observe how the man presently straightens his back, turns back through the door, and disappears into the dusk housed inside. That was it. In another life he might be the odd fellow in the macintosh, who inexplicably turns up in the Hades-chapter in *Ulysses*, or perhaps an escaped prisoner who has not yet understood that death is inescapable. But how would we know? Here he cuts a figure as insignificant and confused as . . . oh, better not to say it.

Let us return instead to where it is happening. Here is the master of the house, a certain Salvatore, stepping toward the bier to speak with his resting guest:

—Are you dead?
—Yes, said Gracchus, so to speak. Many years ago, yes, it must be a great many years ago, I fell from a precipice in the Black Forest—that is in Germany—when I was hunting a chamois. Since then I have been dead.
—But you are alive too, said the Burgomaster.
—So to speak, said the Hunter, in a manner of speaking, I am alive too. My death ship lost its way; a wrong turn of the wheel, a moment's absence of mind on the pilot's part, the distraction of my lovely native country, I cannot tell what it was; I only know this, that I remained on earth and that ever since my ship has sailed earthly waters.

Kafka's hero is like a free floating punctuation mark that has not yet found the sentence to which it belongs and therefore is unable to rest. He is dead but cannot die, living merely "so to speak"—or "comparatively," as we might prefer to say. A fluttering butterfly in a forgotten fold of time. With a name as gray as the jackdaw that in Italian is named *gracchio* (and translated to Czech turns into *kavka*), Gracchus is without point of fixity, in no possession of address. "I am forever on the great staircase that leads upward," he answers when Salvatore asks him if he has any "part in the other world."

> On that infinitely wide and spacious staircase I clamber about, sometimes up, sometimes down, sometimes on the right, sometimes on the left, always in motion. The hunter has been turned into a butterfly.

And there we shall leave him, in the frozen suspension of that single frame, on a podium of air or an altar of nothingness. A butterfly he has become. Perhaps we are dealing with a *Lycaeides melissa samuelis* Nab. with its pale belly and blue wings, or the likewise blue *Lycaeides sublivens* Nab., also known as *Plebejus (Lycaeides) idas sublivens*, which weaves rays of gray into its tinctured attire. Imagine.

§ Four

Or. Rather. Imagine this. Thin thickets of thought, silky spreads and pouting bulks, crisp like the scribble of skates on early winter ice or concourses billowing with bumptious color, gaseous envelopes of fog and fuddle, reticent at first and reserved, merely hissing intent like snakes still sleepy or beggars new and novice . . . then emerging as from cans tracked twisted turned open, lids let loose, inflated like letters growing light and nimble (already running, pandorically, into numbers), sighs stringing stresses to prompt sound and sound hushing syllables into words, breath exhaling cadences to cause clauses and sentences—shyly—no longer so shyly—no longer shyly at all—drawing stretching gushing out, limbs thus becoming entangled, then loins purloined . . . so the vast strange wild abundance of circles, cones, hooks, dots, dashes, and slashes, columns raging tall and thin, may be placed preciously into perspective, like signatures on dotted lines, making their muddled mess, alas, and mist and vapor in masses unimagined, yet remaining what they always were, fuzzy frames of urge and fraud, and slabs, like stabs, that aid and restrain nothing but errant air, winding, grinding, mining, molding, rotating round and around, flitting, floating, and fluttering, trembling like towers twisted or silhouettes stretched straight and straining . . . until suddenly, like a slip of the tongue, they race rapidly astray, evaporating into airs so proverbially thin that our senses are stripped of . . . well . . . yes . . . of aspiration, and eyes are lost in the blank yonder beyond blue . . . that blurry oblivion. . . .

What could this alliterative extravaganza be other than an unexpected unveiling of the shrouded self of gray nihilitic matter? the dim, disorienting heart of our contumacious pursuit? Let us raise the index, saved for closing, for we seem to have come to the last matter at hand, the concluding substance to be tested and treasured, and we wish to signal the event. This, then, is the element we will count as our fourth, last, yes final: the cloud.

Swellings of silver and shadow, clouds possess the secret elasticity of time, the rougish longevity of the alphabet, the soft opacity of thought. They may shape themselves as black bursts of buzzing flies, but also tremble like hissing hazes of memory; they may demonstrate the deft balletic economy of wishful thinking, but also billow like shimmering concoctions of thrill and fraud. Yet whatever their pitch and persuasion, so calm of head, so lax of loin, we suspect these shapes of substance-without-substance can be reckoned with for two things only: they are unfathomable and will not last.

Let us try to corroborate our inkling by sampling a few examples. "You seem to have your head in the clouds," we may point out to the mysterious stranger who suddenly has appeared at our side, as he seems aloof and about to turn blue (detached but not yet dejected). He does not reply, however, evidently being inept in adding those bits to the conversation that might prevent it from limping. A dreamer, as faltering in speech as a suspect, his aim and intent remain, to us, fuzzy. With the smooth sway of a daydreamer, he even seems to recede from presence while still remaining perfectly with us. Whatever his concern, we understand merely that he is preoccupied. Absent in spirit, though there in the flesh. Quite candidly gray. If his eyes were to change to a simmering black, we would understand that melancholy had him in its glistening embrace. In that case, things might still be manageable; clouding over like the memory of a bribed witness, the stranger would be lost to hope and confidence, but at least we would know that much. Most people build on grounds considerably less firm. At present, however, nothing of the sort. Although within sight, our stranger remains outside the radius of our influence, beyond the touch of conscious effort and amicable concern. Remember Achilles? Nebulous, is the word.

Now, let us presume a scenario less lackluster. Imagine that the sun would spill into the streets by the bucket-full, a soft breeze setting the sky apart from the horizon, the birds and trees in folly tatters. There he is now, our stranger, no longer brooding, but "floating" instead on clouds. Perhaps a blaze of amorous flight, suffused in wisps of sunshine, has lifted him out of the prison of earthly existence, framing his life in a gold as pliable as honey, or making it so fluffy to sink into that it transforms itself to the pillow that childhood memories stuff so well. It would not make much difference, though. This state of mind, too, would appear vague and skittish, as solar inebriation might make things more blissfully voluble, but hardly ever clearheaded. Furthermore, our stranger's bevy of amatory bravery would also be shortlived, because when rapture ripens into that which is richer (that is love), oddly enough, it will lead him back to earth again, where we would still be wandering wonderingly. Why?, you may query. Because, we shall answer, love that lasts is rooted. Always always. Like tongue in throat.

Whether signifying free or fettered situations, then, no matter how blue in mind or crimson in concern, clouds are as fleeting in nature as they are in form, and often as beautifully deceptive. They cannot be expected to last. Their game is that of ending; their act one of vanishing. Still, lying there in the grass, observing them from afar while chewing on a solicitous straw, we realize that the surging statues that are being formed so lazily above us seem nonetheless . . . well . . . curiously familiar. "I wandered lonely as a cloud," a well-known congregation of verses declares, before describing how its wanderer dances marvelously without moving a mite:

> For oft, when on my couch I lie
> In vacant or in pensive mood,
> They flash upon that inward eye
> Which is the bliss of solitude;
> And then my heart with pleasure fills,
> And dances with the daffodils.

Well acquainted with the Lake District, its caves, characters, and communities, Wordsworth's solitary traveler remains supine on his couch. (He might as well have been an anonymous somebody, or a gray figure, stretched out on the bed in a dingy hotel room, ruminating on the serpentine flower motif diffused across his bedspread.) Still, he manages to cross continents and oceans faster than both vessel and vehicle. Elongated on a chaise longue or perhaps prone on a crackling mattress, sedately sitting against the cell wall or perched perchance on a grassy slope, yet always alone like the clouds he is watching, the wanderer's thoughts float unfazed by limitations imposed by space and time, free and unhampered, hovering like three-dimensional patterns of cogital vapor. Clouds, then, may be termed familiar by virtue of their affinity with our secret feelings, our hidden thoughts. (Was it not Kierkegaard who, in his short "Eulogy to the Fall," claimed that "there is no better image for clouds than thoughts, and none better for thoughts than clouds—clouds being figments of the brain, and what are thoughts if not that?") Gypsies of meteorology, clouds exhibit no geographic loyalty, but are, merely, unobtainable forms in motion. Yet that is why, of course, they remain so alluring to us, fettered as we are by a chain suspiciously similar to the one connecting 9 and 5: they provide shape to our wildest, most bewildering longing: that for freedom.

> —Now tell me whom do you love most, mysterious stranger? Is it your father, your mother, your sister, or you brother?
> —I have neither father, mother, sister, nor brother.
> —Your friends?
> —You use a term which to this day remains unknown to me.
> —Your fatherland?
> —I do not know on what degree of latitude it is located.

—Beauty?
—I would like to love that, the goddess, the immortal.
—Gold?
—I hate it as you hate God.
—What do you love, then, stranger of strangers?
—I love the clouds . . . the clouds passing by . . . over there . . . over there . . . the marvelous clouds!

Heralds of distance, announcers of space . . . floating there, over there . . . always farther away than any fingertip will be able to tap . . . clouds soak up our moods like wads of cotton . . . Is there a person whose mind has not been crossed by the thought that they—over there—keep the clandestine key to his clamshell heart? Tracing their effusive formations with our eyes, we wonder: there, is that not the face of our beloved? Or there, is that not the soft curve of her hip? There, is that father's marvelous smile? a tousled tree? or some shed robe? Or is it, perhaps, rather the eddy after a diving crocodile? the tremulant rings left by a stone sinking swiftly and diligently, in virtuous silence? And there, are they not horsemen galloping across flatlands? fish moving in air like birds? or whisps of uproarious white in the ebony well of a cup of coffee? Or there . . . there . . . or there . . . . Clouds give shape to human projections. They are three-dimensional embodiments of the celluloid strip of wishes that flickers so brightly on the screen of our thinly layered eyelids. As such, they can be counted on as only the strangest among companions: those who forgive while appearing to forget.

In the *Meteorologica,* Aristotle's "study of what is found above," there is a section treating "the region which lies second beneath the celestial and first above the earth." This nebulous area, it is stated, is "the joint province of water and air, and of the various phenomena which accompany the formation of water above the earth." Among its variations we encounter rain, fog, and cloud, hail, snow, and frost. According to Aristotle, all these phenomena, however varied, ensue from solar revolutions. Depending on its movement to or away from earth, the sun causes composition or decomposition, appearance or liquidation. It is the lord of regeneration and of destruction. The earth is merely a resting matter and its aura of saturated moisture disappears when pierced by the genially ignited rays of multifarious light. As the heat increases and scatters wide and vividly, part of the earth's dampness dissolves in higher regions, like the enchantment of letters when we grow older. As it decreases, the earth is cooled off and condensing dampness changes from air to water, falling as naturally as syllables combine into words in our adult mouth.

> The exhalation from water is vapor; the formation of water from air produces clouds. Mist is the residue of the condensation of air into water, and is therefore a sign of fine weather rather than of rain; for mist is as it were an unproductive cloud.

In contrast to fog, as "unproductive" as counting your blessings in hell, clouds are associated with a certain portent—often of the unhappy kind. They harbor what we do not yet know, but glimpse and brood upon, then begin faintly to suspect, only to end on a note distinctly dark. They contain the vexed promise of concern, worry, grief, or unease . . . something, at any rate, on which we are unable to put our finger, but which we perceive when taking that dim view with which street parlance provides us . . . *quelque chose de grisant* . . . as dismal as the afternoon waiting for us in Friedrich Theodor Vischer's eulogy to inexpression, lackadaisically entitled "Gray Song":

> Why does my stifling soul
> Feel so dull and dense, so faint and feeble,
> When in vain during a gray afternoon
> I torment myself with my books—
>
> When the sky covers my sleepy eyes
> Like an ashen fence, and the eye,
> Far and wide, removed from the beloved blue,
> Cannot discover a trace?
>
> A violin is heard from a distant house,
> Mawkish like a child's drawn-out crying,
> But one hardly notices it,
> T's a thin tone, bored, in the distance.

No winds move, no green cover the field,
Spring is here, but is not able to subdue
Winter's aged streaks of snow
Still running through forest and ditch.

So deserted and still! Only the black bird
Freezing on the ridge of the roof
Gives a drawn-out sorrowful sound,
As if spurring on a disaster soon to come.

I know it well, such a gray afternoon
Is my entire being, all my work and woe.
It is not nostalgia, not pain, not desire,
Words cannot express, the pen not write it.

It feels as if I myself were gray in gray,
Even to complain seems much too colorful.
If life is nothing, if life is something,
No matter how I brood, I am loathe to tell.

Given to moods as forgetful as the wind, that blind heedless phantom, we are only too familiar with such afternoons. Without proper core and particular content, they seem interminable. Vainly we try to occupy ourselves with meaningless tasks—reading a book, perhaps, or permitting our gaze to touch, pierce, then eventually lose itself outside the window—inertly leafing through yesterday's paper—familiar stories, old news—or opening the rumbling refrigerator for heaven knows what time (but alas, nothing unusual has appeared within). February seems to reign firm and feckless in our soul. Clouded over ourselves, "in vacant or in pensive mood," we sense time dragging its feet through the back alleys of our mind. Thusly turning nebulous, we dream ourselves into that depth that, ineptly, has opened up inside our vacuous thoughts. "Gray in gray," or: life lacking lacquer.

If the words we pronounce at that moment; if the sentences we may still move our lips to mouth; if the paragraphs we essay to patch together like mismanaged relations . . . if all of this last lost labor could be made visible, it would still appear merely as concoctions of clouds, shabbily rising out of a glorious gorge. Some fatidic discharge. A *marchand de nuages* as skillful as the cook in Baudelaire's poem "La Soupe des nuages" might be able to salvage the mess we are in, but during afternoons such as these, clouds tend to provide only the smudgy, inexpert promise of rejuvenation. Not much to salvage, and certainly no salvation. We would do well to pull something old over us instead, forgetting past woes and present worries, and simply sleep away an ennui that threatens to become a permanent fixture in our life (like that solitary colorless bulb illuminating the skullscape we term our mind). But sleep, too, seems bland and banal—as if it did not create a break in our boredom, but in fact plotted its continuation. Perhaps we slept earlier and now ought to try to wake up instead? Everything remains uniformly quiet silent sullen, a sluggish day dream without row and rumpus. No nuance, no news. Neither smart surprises, nor splendid shocks. Not a single emission from that unstirred gullet of a stale sky. In fact, the atmosphere remains as irreproachably useless as an old bus ticket. Oh, life is a damper, all right.

During such afternoons it is impossible to decide whether the monotony of existence is everything or "nothing," as Vischer's stack of stanzas sees it. The alternatives seem to amount to the same; life no longer has resolution. Studded with sod and sorrow, we breathe as if living on overtime, in a pocket filled with nebulous negation—that curious *espace meublé* that is "known to us," to take quick recourse to *Ada*, "only as furnished and full even if its contents be 'absence of substance.'" Yet despite having too much time on hand, we are dealing with the opposite of a leapday. It is, rather, as if 24 hours were subtracted from 365 revolutions and we were forced to live through this unyielding minus-period with the detached precision of a watchmaker. The-day-that-did-not-exist-but-still-occurred. Something along a comatose line such as this. A zero added to the almanac, at any rate . . . or a circular nothing penciled on the white leaf of a long forgotten calendar . . . an ovoid absence irregularly introduced among the invariably alert chalk lines on a prison wall . . . literally insignificant, yet still to be accounted for—like Kurd Lasswitz's otherwise mercifully forgotten "novel about a cloud," *Aspira*, set in a Gothic print whose implacable angularity is the very opposite of cloudiness.

Such a nonsensical day, unpleasant as rancid milk, must be inarticulable. "Words cannot express, the pen not write it." Even lament, however lackluster, seems too colorful a manner in which to voice our present situation. The prevailing mood is not that of melancholy, then, really, the charcoaly demon of temperament, but rather one of bland listlessness. No gloom seems involved, no depression, no malaise, no sadness, only flat, faceless destitution—an emptiness impure and simple. As if we were missing ourselves. Which must mean that we experience the expressionless only while waiting—perhaps for vigor to inveigle us or dearth to depress us, power to charm us or death to down us. Anythingaslongasitisnot-*this*. Thus our attention cannot be the waiting of the vigilant; nor the caution of the hurt; not the anticipation of the eager; nor the confidence of the trusting. It seems, merely, the composed lingering of the disillusioned. Dragging, existence has turned into a game of solitaire. Its sole purpose is to kill time, that is to say, to annul the *raison* of its *être*. The pencil lies unused on the table in front of us, considerably shorter, to be sure, than when we found it in one of the dark humming desk drawers sometime ago, but still no more insignificant than our flavorless existence (oh, sham tender finitude). Which might suggest—in fact and turn—that it is not we who project feelings onto cloudy formations, thereby animating them, but rather the clouds that confer features on us by taking them away. If we could muster the strength to throw a glance in the mirror that hangs diffidently in the room in which the pencil is still lying on a table, we would probably look like an erect minus sign. Not much more. Perhaps with a face of contorted vapor maladroitly affixed on top. That *O* without the scream. Filled to the brim with void and silence.

"Seem but the clouds of the sky," Yeats writes in the last stanza of "The Tower,"

> When the horizon fades;
> Or a bird's sleepy cry
> Among the deepening shades.

Such is the story of our life: scattered and squandered among ever deepening shadows.

As time passes, they become omnipresent, these saturated shades making the shapes by which we gather, then lose ourselves. Cargos of pensive transience, they seem to demonstrate a particular affinity with gray literature, appearing in Homer, Aristophanes, and Hamann, Wordsworth, Baudelaire, and Benjamin . . . Brodsky and Ashbery and Jelinek . . . there are some even in Beckett's television play " . . . but the clouds . . . ," in which Yeats's line returns at still longer intervals, as if the passages between the repeated recollections contained their own cloudy temporality: " . . . *W's lips move, uttering inaudibly:* ' . . . clouds . . . but the clouds . . . of the sky . . . ' . . . " And then, gaily, graily:

> I begged in vain, deep down into the dead of night, until I wearied, and ceased, and busied myself with something else, more . . . rewarding, such as . . . such as . . . cube roots, for example, or with nothing, busied myself with nothing, that MINE, until the time came, with break of day, to issue forth again, void my little sanctum, shed robe and skull, resume my hat and greatcoat, and issue forth again, to walk the roads. [*Pause.*] The back roads.

Lying on the couch or in a bunk, resting in the inner sanctum of our mind, dreaming about the nulliverse (this space-time concoction of things thoughts thralls gray), we tend to attribute features, beauteous or horrific, to those floating formations—an ironic corner of the mouth, perhaps, or two peering eyes and a pair of frowning eyebrows—but upon further reflection it is the clouds that invade us, is it not?, wiping out motif as well as motivation. Sooner or later, surely, we pass into that nephelicitous frame of mind in which nothing is kept. grayness occurs. and neutrality prevails.

Do we need proof of this? Hardly with this mist around. Yet for the sake of the reference to Baudelaire earlier, still somewhat scurrilous, let us imagine a hungry person bending over that bowl of hot soup. Let us assume it contains a reddish thicket of borscht, almost levitating in dense dampness. Let us envision how the soup breathes its mask of moisture over our stranger's face. And let us feel the heat. Let us do all this and then ask: is it really he who partakes of the food? Is it not rather the hovering comestible that incorporates him? After all, the stranger's features are slowly being dissolved in the borscht's confusion of red flakes, absorbed by the grated beets' unfathomable embouchement. It may be possible, as Benjamin writes in a reflection on this particular meal, that we are witnessing a "cloud-diet related to manna," but the identity of the person eating is certainly getting lost in the soup's inexhaustible depth. And exactly this is the case with the frame of mind we are presently trying to reframe: it "eats" and besets us, hollows out and empties our mind. We linger and loiter, drift on or about, getting absolutely nowhere. As we watch the ashes of our faltering existence grayen, redden, grayen, as *Watt* put it, we try to make amends by choosing some *mots justes* to sum—no, sop—it all up, but sooner rather than later we feel racked, throw up our hands, and indulge again the simplest of desires known to us: that to disappear.

Around us, clouds, nothing but clouds.

If we are lucky, we realize we can still put on "hat and greatcoat," silently step out of our sanctuary life, and—like Beckett's recluse—promenade along the back roads of existence. Away, just away from it all. What good will words ever do us?

Referring to "the weapons of words," Hölderlin's poem "At the Source of the Danube" speaks of them as the sacred relics that "the sons of fate" left behind. "Often," it is then stated,

> when the holy cloud hovers around us,
> We are seized with awe, unable to explain.

Only one attitude seems possible toward those tussles of fuss and commotion that try to animate an uninvolved sky: awe. With gaping mouth and eyebrows quipped like circumflexes we stand there, "unable to explain." Certainty is no longer part of the picture. Words will do no justice to the situation. The cloud inside which we find ourselves is not only diffuse, then, as if we had borrowed someone else's glasses, but moreover, it does not allow room for explanation. If earlier it had established distance, thus offering the means by which definitions could be created, the cloud now seems to eliminate distinctions. Rather than providing surface for the endless sky extending above and proportion for the dot-like I at its horizon, it dissolves length, measure, volume, ratio, and balance. This must be the cloud of unknowing. Having descended on us like an afterthought. Interpretative strategies will not suffice here, however agile and nimble. They get us nowhere. At most we would be able to assert *that* something is happening in the region now enveloping us like weightless lichenous ectoplasma. But if steps could be found on which we might clamber up toward an allegorical clarity or—rather—crawl downward, cowardly, to security, one cumbersome step at a time, they would in this case convey an ominous similarity to a treadmill. Caught in a motion circular and turning, we would not be able to move from the spot. Even without steps it would be fruitless to attempt to master the situation—by grasping that fluffy vacuity surrounding us, say, believing we could force it like a sleeping bag into its cover or drive it back like a crew of spirits rubbed out of their lamp. Neither push nor shove will be of help. Not any. At all.

If fortunate, we might be able to recall the dim memory of how the same occurrence happened earlier, but that would require relying on a dormant code slushing around the bottom of our mind-barrel, one that blatantly no longer obeys the dictates of firmly poised knowledge. So much for taking an initiative, then. Compass needles are good for nothing; the topography is decidedly different; and the cardinal points have reached a number alarmingly greater than four. There is nothing to do but to face the music. We have lost both dint and direction. Not to mention ourselves.

Perhaps we might be able to escape these present straits if we put our diminutive implement to a more practical use? Yes, perhaps now is the time to raise it as if it were the frozen end twisted off a thunderbolt? Maybe there is even reason to hope such an immobilized snake of suddenness might guide us out of our tensile tangle? Or should we use it, rather, to connect that series of numbered points we envision hanging in the haze like colored pellets or blinking bulbs, a mist of miniscule light buoys prefiguring—why, an unexpected exit, of course. But the picture we would thus be drawing in the air is not likely to represent a free safe-conduct, the last proverbial straw, or a door open enough to permit us a squeezy, if not easy, way out. Rather it would appear to be a closed space, soap-bubbly in shape and all-encompassing, yet without walls, roof, and floor. Provided, of course, we would be able to identify those variegated points tossed out like debris in the air. Oh, they would be neither colored nor blinking, we may be assured, and furthermore, we would probably need another swarm of points, somewhat smaller in size than those already in existence, yet clearly visible, in order to locate the coordinates fitting within the larger picture. And so on into an infinity as eclipsing in kind as the cloud where we are presently stuck. A dotted haze, a miniscule mist of motes. Not a chance, then. And certainly no prospect.

So let us sum up instead. Let us take stock. (Time and fingers are running out.) What we seem to be facing can no longer be the sky's expanding endlessness, that dynamic host of void and distance, little else, but is rather an ever diminishing eternity (shrinking like a block of butter in a frying pan), which nonetheless unfolds within—an infinitesimal greatness, or smallness, whatever we prefer, where each point is a mite more unassuming, a whit less large than the one before, but which still spreads itself out in manners and methods omnipresent. (Something on the order of Josephine's "least possible trace," say.) It is as if each cloud contained another cloud, its dimension smaller, its chunk of mass more modest, but containing its own proper character and specific weight. So searching for security, our gray-in-gray figure (zigzagging yellow still in hand) moves in fact toward an ever increasing uncertainty, lost in a crowded haze, even if its bodily movements could be reduced, finally, to a suspended sedentary position in front of a rectangular surface over which is spread a slew of smaller squares holding even smaller squares captive.

Each cloud thus contains a cloud that contains a cloud. Yes. And provided any section of shapes and shallows, however partial or curbed, will yield the semblance of form, each image, too, must be < an image that must be < an image. Yes, yes. (Tip those smaller-than signs on top of each other and see them disappear within. No? There you go.) Thus every image of a cloud also contains an image of a cloud, and every cloudy image, too, contains a cloudy image. Of course. O. Yes. Droll Sisyphus dressed up in Russian drag. Yet oddly, just as the telescope, with which we witness the latter's eternal labor being thwarted incessantly, consists of links where each section is a trifle smaller in width and length than the previous one, so this doubling (and doubling of a doubling) allows our gaze to stretch itself further, our train of thought to stroll farther . . . wandering . . . wandering over there . . . while concomitantly, the area of their action is, in fact, growing smaller, the domain of their doing ultimately decreasing to the stubborn surface of the tip of that yellow thing. An inverted pyramid, correct? Pnin caught the logic:

> The short pencil, if held obliquely, curved like a stylized snake, but if held vertically became monstrously fat—almost pyramidal.

If we can imagine a style of writing influenced by such troubling movement—expanding while diminishing—where erasures would open up inner horizons; repetitions suddenly expose inscapes of unknown makeup and magnitude; revisions uncover vast vistas of interiority, we would be dealing with a narrative in which plot no longer had precedent. Sisyphus will forever attempt to roll his boulder up to the top of the mountain—having long since forgotten why—but who would, indeed, care? The story is as old as the hills he has yet to master. To the degree that we are able to still talk about "narrative," it would be guided rather by the superimposition of the images concocted. Here it would be, as it were, more important to know who is the neighbor of whom than where the post office is located or from what station the bus departs. Relationships are established at the smallest local level, not across distances as great as the tundras of Caucasus or in the roundabout manner of the night-reveler returning home. Like bees busily sorting out their hive (. . . spirits spurring Mr. Legion . . . djinns thrashing in a bottle . . .), every inhabitant may turn out to be the neighbor of everyone else. Hidden tunnels, secret passages, and clandestine canals, concealed corridors, forgotten routes, and phantom paths produced out of thinnest air—those stock props of suspense—connect all points not necessarily with each other, but with the *possibility* of connection. (Pseudonyms, alibis, and alter egos tend to take care of the rest.)

The order found in such a narrative may indeed seem strange, even hazardous, but it is not without its own consistency. Easiest would be to imagine its particular coherence as made of material sufficiently pliable to be stretched to a certain length. As with rubber-bands, greatest tension occurs with maximum ability to distend. Still, this type of narration contains neither beginning nor ending, which is important, but merely a course determined by the elasticity of the points forming its circumference. Everything proceeds in a sort of springy suspended circularity. And as the rubber band inscribes a vacuum, so this spiral-shaped sequence moves around one and the same jumbly chasm of nullity. Every once in a while the narrative gazes into it as into a well, and at that moment it may tell about memories and myths from times long past. (Children born out of wedlock, feuds among siblings, loyalties tested but proven to endure.) At other times, its eyebrows are sternly knitted as when we examine the empty compartment in a wallet—an activity so sullen and vain, however, it disintegrates like late winter light on granulous snow. Occasionally the void has diminished coolly and competently, now looking like the slit that young boys produce by folding the movie ticket into a model of an almost non-existent groove into which they subsequently whistle, full of expectations of the adventure this prank is supposed to create. Whereas at other times the hole is as slack as the opening on an uninflated balloon—and then the course consists, rather, of nursery tales whose limp character cannot hide the fact that the story-telling parent, with an attention wobblier than jelly, is about to concede his soul to sleep.

In this manner the void may stretch from the old person's satiated memories to the child's unformed pranks, and of course—as now—also form the immaterial middle in a failing account of narrative modes, shaken out of the sleeve like the magician's plastic duck in a circus of modest resources. The plot does not really cohere, but the contract into which we entered when we paid for our seat vouches for a minimum of trust, assuring that the performance will not go unnoticed. And at any rate, soon the brothers Salto will arrive and their tricks hardly are worth nought or nothing.

This, then, is the story concerning the form of narration treated here: no one knows how it will continue, though anyone may make assumptions, anticipate a number or two, or even expose a couple of the easier tricks. It may start with a rubber band and end as a plastic animal in the bathtub, even if occasionally it might also commence by introducing an insignificant item in an old desk and conclude with a question mark as large as a dirty cirrus. The point is that the gist of this narration is as non-thingy as the middle of that rubber band; still it may be fashioned in countless ways. Granted, it lacks both essence and substance, but more important, it possesses form, that unavoidable condition for all narrative. Furthermore, it remains invisible and impossible to ascertain, like an opaque object into which we begin to sink without noticing it—unsteadily bobbing as if in a life-buoy, securely anchored as if in a wedding ring, or royally fitted as the queen's head in her crown. Our grainy void does that. It allows us to perceive and experience an aperture opening orifice toward other worlds, where nebulae may appear as small as fish roe, molecules as unfathomable as parallel universes. It keeps us, that is, in the gray.

If we wish to tell stories in this mode, we must stick to the contour, because security is found only there. Form precedes fact, as matter cannot be emptied of form, whereas the latter easily may manage without the former. Our cavity can assume the shape of a podium, stage, or manege where life's drama is being played out, but we will be able to tell about it only as long as we remain seated in the bleachers. Hence we are forced to remain floating as we grasp the single straw at our disposal: relationality. Images must lead to other images like the days in a calendar, chinks of a chain, so explanations, too, must feed other explanations. We ought not to cast our pebbles into that well, therefore, and under no circumstances the worn coins of wishful dreams, because above its hollow halo—or rather through it—invisible threads as thin as cobweb are currently being spun, and it is this frail feeble pattern—a lattice work of unapparent connections, stealthily created links, chinks, and liasons, secretly knotted ties—that gives us the required feeling of tension, tautness, and now. To narrate is to walk on water.

Nabokov issues the warning:

> A thin veneer of immediate reality is spread over natural and artificial matter, and whoever wishes to remain in the now, with the now, on the now, should please not break its tension film. Otherwise the inexperienced miracle-worker will find himself no longer walking on water but descending upright among staring fish.

Let us end by emphasizing what already is abundantly clear: if blue narration sinks at all, it sinks into dreamy waters drifting as faithfully as the fish that, wondering in frozen attention about the sudden visit of memory, now wriggle on hunting other food, other thought (here a quick bonus example, culled from V.N.'s short story "Lik": "a world of ineffable tenderness—a bluish, delicate world where fabulous adventures of the senses occur, and unheard-of metamorphoses of the mind"); its gray counterpart, in contrast, attempts to steam the water's mirror, reading, in its complicitous graying, evaporating patterns drawn like creases in a non-existent palm. Will it stay cupped and keep alive?

As a consequence we do not ask what is being told, but how. And therefore it remains unimportant (but not uninteresting) to ascertain what a cloud, for example Hölderlin's, represents, and becomes more meaningful to examine how it signifies—or rather unsignifies. Linguists observe this distinction by using a notation we will adopt without further ado. If a "cloud" refers to an atmospheric phenomenon, characterized by a certain moisture that may form as quickly as it disappears, then a /cloud/ written between slanting lines as narrow as train compartments on Friday afternoon identifies the function of this something within a larger system of signs—it concerns, that is, its role as signifier. What and How, that seasoned tandem. If the phenomenon's features play the main role in the former case, in the latter they are less important than extras in a documentary devoted to overpopulation.

Let us turn to an example that, at first, seems to have little in common with Hölderlin's holy cloud: Jane Austen's *Emma*. On a central but concealed place in the book—almost like the forest glade before we found it—Harriet shows the book's heroine a couple of trifles she has preserved because they remind her of a man they both know and with whom she secretly has been in love. Among the bric-à-brac, she picks out one half of a "court plaister" the other half of which had been used by the object of her admiration when he cut his finger with Emma's penknife. Later, however, Harriet also shows her friend a sharpened-down writing implement. "It was the end of an old pencil," writes Austen, "the part without any lead." (In the past, we hasten to insert in a whisper whose theatrical tone we have no time to dissimulate, it was not unusual that only the pencil's lower part contained graphite. The reason, of course, was parsimoniousness: when the utensil had been whittled down to a certain length it was difficult to use, and since wastefulness was to be avoided, this portion was denied the dwelling dignity of graphite.) Unlike the half plaister, Harriet's blunt blurt of a pencil had belonged to the man she loved. He had rejected it when he sat down to make a few notes on how to brew spruce beer. Borrowing another pencil from Emma, he had left the useless stump "upon the table as good for nothing." In Harriet's amorous eyes, though, it promised a value greater than its weight in any metal, precious or not.

Let us take a look at this stoic implement that hardly deserves that quarter of a name it still carries on one side. Granted, it may no longer be serviceable as a pencil; consisting of an oblong wooden sheath with a lock, it clearly lacks the black vein that would make it a bit-of-blood utensil. In that sense it is "good for nothing" and reduced to the least possible trace. But it has yet to complete its course through the story. Evidently, Austen's pencil is still able to signify an object of wood that most likely hails from the area around Keswick, has a certain size, and at one time was formed around an inner cavity filled with a substance consisting of carbon, rubber, glue, and a few other components. The only strange aspect is that it no longer serves its purpose (well, all right: nor, indeed, does it serve its point). Other than that, nothing remarkable. A pencil is a pencil is a pencil, also when it, like Harriet's, hardly amounts to one.

If we instead examine Austen's /pencil/, however, we discover that we no longer are dealing with small checkered items on a questionnaire with the heading *What*: kind of wood (❏ pine ❏ ash); type of graphite (❏ Borrowdale ❏ Keswick); bluntness (❏ significant ❏ insignificant); general serviceability (❏ good ❏ bad). Or even amorous memories, nostalgic reminiscences, or the intimacies girl friends confide to each other (see enclosure). Rather, Austen's /pencil/ constitutes one of many intersections in a network of functions entitled *How*. It is, laboriously put, a differential sign in a semiotic system. Which means, merely, that it lacks significance of its own and can function only in relation to other similarly conditioned likes. If "pencil" is a term standing for a content, /pencil/ is a signifier that, in the manner of a secret agent, operates in an area where only dismay and discrepancy exist.

In Austen, this other territory of thought and telling consists of pairs contrastingly coupled as desire/loss, expectation/disappointment, then/now, and stay/continue. Thus we ought not to be surprised that Harriet, with an ambiguous air of despair and readiness (as if, for the umpteenth time, pushing a strand of hair away from her face), finally decides to throw her memories on the fire. For the idealist this is the only way to descend dry-footed from a cloud of unknowing. No ladder is better than destruction. Ever the good materialist, the soberer Emma distinguishes between the two treasures. Determining the utility of the former, the futility of the latter, she explains: "I have not a word to say for the bit of old pencil, but the court plaister might be useful."

If objects in Emma's world are defined by the purpose they might proclaim, one based on the meaning conventionally attributed to them, the objects in Harriet's world are determined by the function they fill in a world of inner realities. Emma is a pragmatist, Harriet an idealist—even if they redefine these categories with the same freedom the pupil assumes when he plays hooky from the philosophy lecture. In both cases, the pencil remains a "pencil."

For us who share Austen's world, however, what counts is not what the pencil is, but how it circulates within the story. No matter how full of details and indications a story might be, without an idea of how these points are to be connected, the text is less interesting than yesterday's shopping list or the inventory of a prisoner's wardrobe. A point becomes important only in relation to others, a fact that the semiologist would formulate in the thesis that they are defined by their difference from each other.

In Sherlock Holmes, we may find a telling example of the sense for signs and their kinship required here. One day around the turn of the century the detective was asked by a tutor to resolve who among this man's pupils had been cheating. Hilton Soames—thus the tutor's name—assumed that one of the boys had sneaked into his room and copied the questions for an exam scheduled for the following day. Finding "several shreds of a pencil that had been sharpened," as well as a broken point, Soames drew the conclusion that "the rascal had copied the paper in a great hurry, had broken his pencil, and had been compelled to put a fresh point to it." But who was it? Holmes is given the chance to exercise his considerable acumen. After having examined the broken point and the crude splinters of wood, he declares:

> "The pencil was not an ordinary one. It was above the usual size, with a soft lead, the outer color was dark blue, the maker's name was printed in silver lettering, and the piece remaining is only about an inch and a half long. Look for such a pencil, Mr. Soames, and you have got your man. When I add that he possesses a large and very blunt knife, you have an additional aid."

Neither Soames nor Watson understand how the master detective is able to draw such conclusions merely by looking at squandered wood shavings and the bluntly broken point of graphite. With a certain impatience Holmes holds up a splinter on which the letters *NN* still can be seen (not for the first time, nor for the last) followed by an empty space, and he explains for those less generously endowed:

"You are aware that Johann Faber is the most common maker's name. Is it not clear that there is just as much of the pencil left as usually follows the *Johann*?"

Holmes reads the object's history in the traces of its destruction. Waste, debris, refuse—everything that the cheated teacher and the obtuse physician automatically consider unessential, and therefore overlook, provide him with the necessary facts. This attention to the genuinely insignificant—that which signifies despite all signs to the contrary, that is, in spite of itself, too—we would now like to conclude, constitutes the one rule of thumb that can be counted on when operating in areas termed gray.

Before we lose this train of thought, helpless yet agog, we would do well to follow the lean wafts of vapor and void still trailing above us and see if we can extricate from them a few lingering characteristics that separate blue narratives from gray. Imagine, for example, well . . . imagine, let us say, a series of agreeably gleaming, delicately poised stones whose carefully chosen order is determined by each member's individual weight, size, and degree of attractiveness in addition to its placement in a larger context we might term, for facsimile's sake, a necklace. Everything seems carefully balanced, pleasingly ordered, tastefully proportioned. Delighted, we are led from one luminous facet to the next, touched by that precious moment of perception when atoms are recombined into a new take on existence. What sparkling rapture. What genial vibrancy. Here and there, we may perceive an inkling of a connection that subtly ignites the relation between the third stone's refined shimmer and the fifth stone's soft reserve (is there a secret? is it a sign?), the fourth's sedulous surface and the eighth's calmer coloration (merely a flicker, but a twinkle), yet on the whole, and vastly more important, what attracts us is not this aspect or the other, but the overall impression made by such lucid arrangement, and of course the irresistable finesse with which the stones seem to gravitate, in graceful unison, toward the middle stone's calm and courteous prism (so gentle, so absorbing). Elated yet peaceful, we are thus happy to bow to the confidence with which we now notice the clasp welding together beginning and end, seemingly without both seam and effort. This is polish; this is finish. This is effortless perfection.

If what we have created in front of our vision is an image for the compositional dash and dexterity characteristic of blue narratives as they steal into our heart with comely smoothness, in the case of their gray counterparts we are dealing with, at best, a pocketful of flat pebbles, democratically alike and all possessing the same status in our pouch's far from illustrious union. Yet despite the dearth of interest and lack of distinction, taken together, believe it or not, these granitic trifles make for a melee of multifariousness—tessalating changes and curiosities that have the pebbles' very lacklusterness to thank for their inexhaustibility, or, if not the stones' uniformity, at least the equality of their functional value. Each pebble may play the part, that is, of another, creating liaisons beyond the confines of control and reaches of intention. Such lambent confusion. Such indolent gleam. We may surmise, then, that in a gray narrative, what counts is supposition, chance, and profusion, not appeal, polish, or seduction. Still there is order here, too, though it is based not on aesthetic refinement but on accidental juxtaposition—those temporary ties caused by a distracted hand twisting and turning in a pocket.

If we were asked to heap into words the law governing this latter kind of narrative, a note in *The Titan* would come in handy. Let us fish it out; it is a gem. At one point in his novel, in an aside dated January 20, Jean Paul mentions an *Erzählspiel*, or a "narrative game," consisting of

> a story which is begun but constantly interrupted, so that one may thus, by one person after the other, be offered a strange, unfitting, multicornered stone which must be included into it, but which often adds to the story in ways utterly at odds with it.

If a blue narrative is based on contexts and consistencies as lustrous as newly waxed floors, a gray narrative, by contrast, is founded on a tottering medley of

interruptions
diversions
intermezzos
digressions
changes
revisions
amendations
lacunae
deviations
insertions
delays
pauses
parentheses
. . .
additions

—much in the manner, in fact, of a punctured bicycle dragged across cobblestones. If anything, we are dealing not with text but with texture, not visions but revisions, not reveries of seamlessness, but dreamy jumbles of "topsy-turvical coincidence," as John Shade put it, that patchily patterned lingual labyrinth whose pleated topography is continuously shifting, steadily changing, yet stealthily still staying the same. Which does not mean that nothing leads to anything, that each statement merely stumbles on a crack and wreaks havoc among the sheathed suppositions still in store, or even less that zero is claimed and then reasserted with an inflated swagger and a misplaced grin, but merely that the premise for gray narratives is the fractures of a story and not its finish. They deal in those *d* things: deceit, desire, and disjunction . . . destabilization . . . dissimulation . . . distance and duplication . . . what Shade termed "plexed artistry" . . . so that the already told is bunched up at every turn of the story, a pleated gathering of gray petals suddenly producing again a flower (however deconstrued). We can no longer be surprised, then, if our crooked implement, with its dull luster of a point and rubbery *daimon* in tow, seems to correspond better to the type of narrative we have in mind (always ready to knock together versions of life out of vapor and motion) than the light, limber pen that discharges its inky delights as beatifically as the morning sun, with an air of silken alertness, spills its splendid seeds into half-awake streets.

Before this curious utensil leads us to what Shade termed an "involute abode," that hazy, rubbery habitat that expands with such smooth monotony, we would like to add a few words about clouds—in particular, the one described by Hölderlin. Although he states in "At the Source of the Danube" that the cloud is "holy," at this point, it seems more significant that its inscrutability (like Achilles's by the ocean) causes wonder. Perplexed, we feel as if the cloud has created a chasm in the sky that up until now looked so familar, yet immediately settles itself over the rupture thus revealed. Wound and plaster. Such a blurry breach, we would now like to conclude, is nothing if not nebulous: coy and somewhat abstruse, affecting that air of diffident fakery, it remains palpable only in the faint fashion of an intuition. This is the moment, of course, when our grayening thoughts ought to totter up from their knees and climb the slope of suspicion—but alas, they will manage merely to slip on its surface and recede into a crack of vanity. Better not try, then. For in the same way the skin on a lemon slice will dry and shrivel shortly after we have cut it, this breach, too, protects the opening that it simultaneously marks. And like that citric membrane, it remains ungraspable as a specter, with shapes of another world shining through with tacit and luring, yet utterly deceptive cohesion.

For Benjamin, such a zone of marked indefinition—flat but roomy—resisted explication. Considering Kafka's parables to be their most exemplary form, he argued that the obstacles and complications crowding them transformed interpretation into an "endless task" that might be compared, most properly, to a trial where the sentence is postponed indefinitely. (Which, of course, does not make the accused less but rather more guilty, as his miserable existence is the true reason for all delays.) Terming them "cloudy spots," Benjamin detected a particularly unsettling example in the parable "Before the Law." In this text about a man from the country who is visiting the courts, no key is given that might provide him with the answer to the question of the origin of or access to the laws. Kafka's incorruptible doorkeeper is standing stern and solid, through thick and thin, Monday after Monday. Only an "endless series of reflections" is offered, but the visitor, jovial if meddlesome, is not treated to true entry. And so it is with us:

> The thoroughly precise singularities which fill the life treated in Kafka's work can be understood by the reader only as tiny signs, suggestions, and symptoms of shifts which the author senses pushing their way into all contexts without himself ever being able to fit into the new orders thus established.

Confronting Kafka's parable, approaching but never quite arriving at a conviction concerning its point, we, too, seem to be facing a perfectly fascinating, furtively enticing, yet adroitly unyielding obstacle. Indeed, only awe and retelling seem to remain as viable options for those thusly gray in gray—in addition, of course, to "groping about" in the text ("with care, with caution, with suspicion") as in, did we not guess it?, a "cloud."

If now we were to write /cloud/, thus, it would not be in order to force into some stable shack the unruly content of our concerns, for example, in the manner of the terminal part of a leg into new footwear (after all, the slanted lines do not suggest shoe horns), but merely to indicate that even clouds have ways in which to convey meaning without betrayal. Such lead is, of course, gelid and afloat—

                                        hovering

   fluttering

                          gliding

            drifting

                                              shifting

      trembling

                       and shaking

—but occasionally, if the distance and climate are just right, we may also point to it, tracing its remote contours with our trained, if tremulous index. Less roundaboutly put, it is possible to track the movements of a /cloud/ through a text—to trail its passage along the generous width between chapters or narrow gaps keeping sections apart, to observe its placid repose above a particular paragraph (while the shadow it casts fuses with the scripted heaps of movement performed by those ant-like creatures below) or to eye it breathing in a syllable, stirring in a sentence, dissolving in a word. Then we will notice everywhere that a /cloud/ makes functions more fleeting, certainty less clear, patience more needed. Vibrating and effusive, it is as much a movement of recollection as it is a fading into oblivion. While it may gather memories the way a mirror will collect light, or a stone its heat, sooner or later it is bound to stretch out, thin and twist, then curl a while, before abandoning that spirituous scatter of structure and vanishing for ever. So "finally," as Baudelaire remarks in his *Curiosités esthétiques*,

> all these clouds appearing in brilliant and fantastic forms, these chaotic shadows, these green and rose plains, floating side by side, these blessed crucibles and firmaments of black or violet silk (crumpled, wrinkled, tattered), those grieving horizons or streams of tempered metal—all these grave and glossy greatnesses show themselves in our innermost as a captivating drink or with the eloquence of opium. A strange circumstance: not for a single moment do we regret the absence of people in front of this fleeting, fugitive magic.

A strange circumstance, indeed. To be alone, thus, is to be summoned by the trim, throaty waves of forgetting, then immersed in their "fleeting, fugitive magic." That is: to become clouded. That is: to grayen. That is, then, to lose yourself, too. *Q.e.d.* We when we-less.

Let us designate forgetting's particular manner of signifying as /gray/, therefore, and let us proceed by saying that it can be neither tears, smoke, gravel, or cloud, nor even a nasty lick of memory loss or a severe spell of distraction, eclectic absentmindedness or downright negligence; rather it must amount to their gradual dissolution. Furthermore, let us assume that /gray/—like burned-out light bulbs, empty dryers, or battered carbon paper—at best will give us an inkling of the absence of what we seek, but also that we cannot trust it to provide us with the correct indication. All surface play and zero seriousness, it forges likeness where none may exist, creating alliances between entities as foreign as sugar and salt or piss and potables. Such similarities never last. Nor do they, thank heaven, tend to take hold. Occurring *between* rather than *as* words, a bit of blurring fluff bolstering a contention otherwise too bumpy and barren, like the cotton candy wrapping its wooden stick, /gray/ demonstrates little persistence of its own. Yet the cloudiness it promulgates . . . crowding the cleft not between cloud and "cloud," but between "cloud" and clue, thus not matter and medium but medium and motion, granting us bounties of deception and abundance of sense (but neither dint nor direction) . . . resembles resemblance, perhaps—yes, that might be it, for /gray/, whatever else it is, seems, well, to be the volatile swelling that secures the shapes by which we get to know things. Appearing only in passing, its hazy momentum lasts merely as long as a row or a ruse, and the lushness it lets loom is peculiar to dream and dissolution.

Now, re the "hazy, rubbery" allusion left suspended a few paragraphs back: what if this /gray/, while sly and silvery sweet, a waste none too hazardous, would acquire density and distinction, like spots of spurious spirit? thus become cloud trying to turn word and not word growing cloudy? This is not the question of questions, oh no, not the quizz of presence or puzzle of quiddity, that Horatian query haplessly wondering (hands wringing) how clouds—passing—never lasting—always vanishing, appearing, then revanishing—might be seized, snatched, or abducted (like fair-haired princesses or that magical moment between fingers that is . . . well . . . that was . . .) . . . no, no, it is not *that* hat, old as Merlin's, and just as inflated, but merely a question whether interior spaces might be shaped, inner domains wrung, or areas simply given air and altitude . . . a granulous etherdome . . . to which they, the clouds, transient trains of flow and escape . . . there, over there . . . nomads of wonder . . . somehow someway somewise might belong. A manner of happening, therefore, remember?, no more, merely a matter of mouth, like the solitary child's pitter-patter of pulmonary rapture on a kitchendoor window thirty years ago, a hovering hue on a blank or black base, say, or wisps of white volatility producing clueless clamor, transitoriness trimmed and toned, thus, and unceasing impermanence. For if they were able, would they perhaps not also breed the lissome letters of indigo ardor or cast ebony shadows of longhand yearning? signal the sly stirrings of the illicit, red like rushing candor, or declare new tidings as pristinely as only the white digit of the blameless do?

Indeed. Of course. They would. Just recall those varicolored fellows in action whom we met in a blue memoir (and who are now distributed, incidentally, among divers characters in books "to keep fictitious children busy" (thus "Mademoiselle O")). Yet, whether scribble of desire or scrabble of deceit, these fumescent reservoirs of grain; those fiberous sources of fog; such fillings of shred, speck, and smog . . . must also augur the dissolution of letters and the disintegration of type; thus, they are bound to contain metamorphorical marvels in bolder, more reckless forms, in which surviving traces of saying will mingle like one-legged misfits, dubious invalids, and lazarean leftovers with the spectral emissaries of another—"hazy, rubbery"—power, sporting ruby-colored robes and moving in manners reminiscent perhaps of death. Not a company to be trusted. But what can we do? Already acquainted, the parties are now doing their bit of dexterous scuff and shuffle on the white floor, and surely, the damage will soon be done. Just take a look. Presently—over there—fuzzy frames of fancy are being formed in a *pas de deux* in which the dunce can no longer be distinguished from the dance, nor the dance from the dust kicked up with such diligent delight. Knocked out of shape by a peculiar kind of demise, these mergers of ignorance and motion carry with them neither content nor resolution, but only the gravid signs of shudder coming and commotion. And so, yes, alas, yes, such clouds must be a hue wee spick or speck violet—and pregnant with thunder.

Why, we are speaking, of course, of the vapor wrought by erasers.

Let us pursue the impotent fog thus invoked. It shows an affinity, it seems, with a particularly equivocal form of violation, hardly unknown to gray literature, which we would like to scrutinize as it might bring our pursuit, finally, to "the terrible, eternal why" of which Baudelaire spoke so many pages ago. Again, we shall turn to Benjamin for assistance.

Confronted with certain books in his childhood dreams, Benjamin would pause on their threshold. In these volumes of yesteryear, he noted later, it always "thundered. To open one would have led me into the midst of the womb, in which a changing and gloomy text clouded over, pregnant with colors." A sphere gone atmospheric, that is, riddling and vague, though real, too, and ominous at that, a clandestine chamber and pellucid womb, through which a wind—wail—whisper—of shiftiness wafts, a tender trace of violence. (This, surely, must be our kind of abode?) If colors emerged "out of gray," according to Benjamin's remark inspected earlier, here they were casually and wrecklessly

> bubbling and flowing, but always turning into a violet that seemed to stem from the interior of an animal for slaughter. Unnamable and as laden with meaning as this outlawed violet were the titles, every one of which appeared to me more peculiar and intimate than the previous. Yet before I could make sure of the first, I awoke without once in the dream having even touched upon the old children's books.

What is "this outlawed violet," so tranquil and treacherous, staining the atmosphere and tainting the action? Is it not the sign of that peculiar violation, always enacted and retracted, that is reading and that is awakening? To stand on the threshold of childhood reverie, poised on the door jamb of an initial subjunctive ("would have led"), having neither opened, nor read the books imagined in the would-be of dreaming, yet knowing the fatal consequences of entering tomes as cavernous as these—hence the gloom that clouds over Benjamin's recollection. And hence the gloom clouding his text. Tainting the grays of fitful remembrance with the plain seductive stain of violet, foreboding shudder like flashes in pans, the shadow it casts, the dimness it diffuses, the vagueness it uses already mark and muddle the opening of this sinister scene, ambiguously collating a book unread with the knowledge of its interior. Closed but somehow examined, known yet never quite confronted, the text remains inaccessible, but continues to enthrall.

Clouded over,
           fusing and confusing,
                      it, no less than its reading, is "unnamable." Remote yet always at hand, the text carries its illegible legend as if crossed-over or struck-through, barring entry to the knowledge out of which it nonetheless must speak. Ominous oddity, that, and dense with dissension. We are seized by awe, but unable to explain. Like an interior made known but not available, "laden with [a] meaning" it does not expose, absorbing and wavering, this is the site of violation. Said to be "unnamable," thus named and disfigured, it is, itself, always already violet—like those dissident shreds of eraser, of course, resting in corpulent clouds of graphite.

Among the documents treating such rubbery, thundering matter, the figure of "Don Miguel de Unamuno" in Miguel de Unamuno's *Niebla*, a book densely downy in duplicity, spells out—thus unclouding and expelling—the double-dealing demonery of /gray/ that matches semblance with dissemblance and parity with disparity. Explaining that "you do not get anywhere by calling things names," he claims, and with appropriate distinction, that "it is my part to indefine and confound." *Indefinir, confundir*... such seems to be the surreptitious injunction, violet and violent, of the artifices performed by that carrotine hood capping a pencil. Fusing and confusing, clouds are the shape in which its feats of indefinition appear. You do not enter us—this their promise—thus their threat—lest you forfeit access. Forge and forget. Ever so /gray/.

Thus it remains, merely, for us to search in their traces and follow behind, attentive like Holmes or apprehensive like a blind man tapping his world into existence with a cane. For as already noted, only the manner in which /gray/ moves through a text seems to put us on track. Yet sooner or later—we have sensed it for a while, but now we know for certain—this quest is bound to end like everything else: in forgetting. A miserable affair, it is, shabby as worn hotel sheets. The older we get, the more laborious the task to keep fresh that cunning scent of the trail; the more memories and indices we have gathered, the easier it is to get lost—so in the end, the longer we have sought, the clearer we seem to forget. What was intended to put an elegant end to our labor turns out to be an impasse. Suddenly standing there, facing a solid fire wall in a remote back alley of our mind, we tap at the bricks in the vain hope they will relax and reshuffle, and eventually reassemble into the eager shape of a gate. But instead oblivion spreads across the surface like mad mutinous ivy, and soon we lose sight of the stones' regular pattern that until a while ago seemed as familiar as the icy thrill in a renegade tooth. Instead . . . instead what? . . . instead the scene turns mute and milky . . . .

Oh, where are we? How did we get here? What will we do? Is this the proverbial "it," a.k.a. the end and the limit, that last lethal stop as unconditional as a full period? But why, why, why? There is something odd and slightly chilly in the façade, at least as faced from where we stand, as if blood was leaving it the way rats desert a ship. Perhaps we have come upon the back of a shadow? some quadrilateral, swiftly dappled extension of ether, ail, and ash? or is it merely the glaucomous gleam of a sheet recording—ah, let us say lunar impuissance? Our eyesight has dimmed and thickened as when flour is scattered over water, so we cannot tell. If only . . . no. Even turning up the volume on our hearing aid, installed, a while ago, behind one of the auricles in what was thought to be an auspicious move (but which, alas, only managed to earmark our failing), proves of little help. And handle? Even less of that. What *is* this pale ply of an appearance, then—think, think, think—oh, yes . . . wait . . . well, might it not be the "spectralness" of which Melville once spoke (tone borrowed, voice stolen), that ghostly rectangular reflection that holds the facets of imagination in a grip firmer than the one in which corsets once tightened the bodies of women, yet lighter than the air their lungs still managed to inhale? "To analyze it", he observed, "would seem impossible." Indeed. Sure thing. We concur. That much appears beyond dispute. Yet, as Melville continued to ask, perhaps we can nonetheless

> hope to light upon some chance clue to conduct us to the hidden cause we seek?

To light upon . . . some chance clue . . . to the hidden cause . . . how could we hope to perform such a miracle with this incandescent surface in front of us, containing everything but being itself, surely, nothing, growing skin across its void in the manner of warm milk cooling . . . how might we, we wonder, happen upon a clue . . . how might—if not by raising our tremulous cane, stick, stem, index, whatever, and do our brutal best to stir that lair of frozen air a little while longer?

Left to our diminishing devices, we thus (1) shake our head; (2) tremble with senile eloquence; and, yes, well, (3) insignify. They do not amount to much, these spasms of finicky plasticity, but at least they may suggest an imitation of our implement's preferred form of action (a proxy from which resolve has left without supervision). More we cannot hope for. What is thereby brought about is insignificance, fine, or rather not so fine, but at least it is similar in manner and mien to the way in which /gray/ intends. And at this point, that is all we could wish to demonstrate. /Gray/ is, after all, not directed like a nanny's good will, the pedagogue's clarifying pointer, or a bowman's callous arrow, but remains rather blunt and wobbly, staggering as if not knowing on which foot to stand, involuntary like a slip of the tongue. It cannot be mastered. Trembling, it will cause merely more fog and further mist. (Neutral voiceover, mildly amused: Hardly helpful, that stirring, then; rather like playing into the hands of forgetting. Why not stay cooler?) If Steinbeck, in a diary note, argued that "the paper eats up pencil line," thus assuming that thickness and density determined how much granulous graphite would get stuck between those white angular teeth, for us . . . ah, for us it is as if the lines intersecting on this elastic surface had been cracked and torn, chomped and munched, until left was only the jumble of mumble in which figures might vanish without loss or notice. Some doddering blotch. But it is OK. We are used to it by now. That blurring oblivion. We are in it.

. . .

Why, you ask?

Because, we must answer, of the vulgar equality of erasers.

Starting to sink into the cupped crevasse of rubbery forgetting, gradually doused in the kind, tomb-like stillness engendered when sleep begins to intercept one's dreams, leaving only faint weaves of soundproof blankness, we finally begin to feel relaxed—as if something vital were giving way, but we knew resistance would prove futile. Ah, the sham tenderness of a cloud! Slowly sinking, we have only wonder left—wonder and perhaps a slight remnant of distracted concern whether, in the words of a master disappearer, we may not, after all, have overestimated

> The transparence and soundness
> Of such an unusual coffin.

Thus, quick, before oblivion whisks consciousness away, let us freeze-frame the setting one last time and consider the tumultuous scuffle of air surrounding us—that nebulous composite of undone dust and debris of old fancies that has haunted us for far too long. Yes, we wish to see if we cannot extricate, in this tangle created by such maldexterous longing, a final thread of sense to which we might latch on and tie our last vanishing hope (an apropositional epitaph, perhaps, with that stripy gleam to it). Focusing our attention like a stray, self-centered wind, we shall perhaps even be able to surge out of our vertiginous verticality for a moment long enough to slip through the shamble of a gate that just materialized in the cloud's midst . . . but wait, no . . . no, that will not do. The inlet is hardly solid enough to be trusted. Just look at those crestfallen portals with beams still being shuffled like cardboard architecture and colors all runny and aflush. Entering, we would lose whatever momentum we have left and die a scattering death in a clutter of sad-colored timber. Next suggestion, please. Well? Yes? Over there? Perhaps instead we could climb through the open window that suddenly has come alive on the first floor, a thin quiver rippling across its solemn countenance (as if to humor our endeavor with amusement bravely kept in check). No, no. That will not do, either. Surely, with an oh-so-fat thud we would tumble down onto a couch screeching like rusty scythes of lightning stashed away in an Olympian tool shed. See? We would only be producing noises that give our final efforts away. That will not do at all. Other ideas? Someone? No? Really? Well, then . . . if we may. . . . Let us simply clear a way for ourselves, perhaps through the side door here to the left, an opening that must have been available all along although nobody has informed us of its existence. But, yes. There is a door here, all right. We can feel the calm cool of its handle as we now dispose our digits around it. Of course, it will turn out to be locked, we may be certain of that . . . see? . . . but at least the key is still snoozing in the lock (a poetic license that ought to have been revoked a long time ago). So, if we could just turn it with a whit of a jerk—simultaneously whitening three finger nails—we might, in fact, be able to make it out of this phantom tumble of a fumble.

There. Done. Now close the door, please. That is it. Well, well. We are inside. Having entered with shoes soled with lead. Now we may cautiously clear our throat and begin to articulate—
hello?
helloo . . . ?
hellooo-o . . .
—but as we grope our way forward, with apologetic feet and hands protruding like undisciplined bundles of dread, we come to understand that silence reigns unchallenged here. Each heaving step is absorbed like an explosion of laughter in a soft cushion ever so obliging. Not a sound. Not a soul.

Let us wait a while, therefore, to allow vision to catch up and confidence to transform these shaky limbs into ours again. There. At last. (Really, they must have belonged to different people.) In the tongue-tied dusk in front of us, we may now begin to make out the contours of an old elevator with one of those "Out of Order" signs slung around its door knob like a bib. Curious. If this had been a dilapidated castle covered in ivy and surrounded with an immobile moat, a shut and barred hotel by an ocean (drab and depressing), or an apartment house from the mellow end of a century—a building, at any rate, where the light in the stairwell has burned out like misfired longing and nobody has bothered to replace the bulb (the torn curl of luciferous metal a sterile reminder of animation), or screwed it in wrongly, or removed it for whatever reason, then we would have been able to make out a list of names, some of them perhaps faintly familiar, tucked away in the penumbra of the portal, discovered in the dusty ledger on a counter, or found on a directory immediately inside the door. In this anonymous register—to be considered, of course, as *N. N.*'s catalogue—we might find, to cite some samples semi-sighted and semi-invented:

a retired cutter by the name of Borrowdale, who polishes his big bald head every morning as if it were a brass bowl; Virgules something-or-other, a comatose gutter worker; the widow Deschamps with her neurasthenic son; a certain C., who lives in the basement; Mr. Null with leaden cheeks and soiled tie; the missionary Dr. Gracchus, an amateur mountaineer, who thirteen years ago was reported lost and whose sister (second floor) later commissioned a cenotaph in his honor; incontinent Mr. Molloy, who prefers to socialize only with H. (or is it A.?) Person, a shady figure one flight up; professor Konrad Gesner, also known as "the father of bibliography" and a "German Pliny," whose *De rerum fossilium lapidum, etc.* contains the illustration that started a course of investigation of which ours is but a vestigial trickle; Miss Frank hiding in the attic; *Frau* Stein; M. and R. Usher, siblings haughty as lamp posts; Salvador Rivas, Sr., a Mexican and father of a former shepherd—Salvador Rivas, Jr.—who is now the concierge in the house across the backyard (the latter's children usually play there, tossing dice, repairing bikes, jumping rope); Lady E. D., who prefers to dress in white and always sports an umbrella; the phantomatic Sineusov, easily confused with Adam von Librikov, a retired lepidopterist whose mark of nobility is as contrived as his German origin; Mr. Leer with daughter; the beautiful S*** presently in the arms of her lover, a hackneyed *artiste* by the name of Leo Tager (alias Caran d'Ache); Detlev Holz, journalist and critic, immaculately dressed, who presently is looking for his watch, but finds merely straw in his pockets; Mademoiselle O., a ravishingly rotund, retired French teacher; Scardanelli (magician); the primadonna Josephine Mauser, secretly admired by *gaspodin* Pnin on the ground floor; and finally Achille Myrmidones, a former athlete of Greek origin who is fond of drinking with Zorro and Zero Salto, two circus artists occupying the adjoining apartment. If perchance we have forgotten someone—like Hilton Soames, for example, the absentminded high school teacher, Har and Em, or enigmatic E. Tranger on the roof—it does not matter much, because, surely, they have been wise enough to leave this counterfeit setting long ago.

Yet, of course, most likely no directory was found in the hall, not in this building, at any rate, and anyway, most certainly we managed to step onto the wide spiral staircase before even noticing there might have been room for inventing one. With our hand flapping for a much needed support of rail among intermittent darknesses (queerly fuzzy to the touch), we slowly suggest ourselves upward, one deracinated step after another, before, all of a sudden, we feel our foot bruising the air, unprepared for that nonexisting, velvety twelfth step of the flight. A current of exquisite panic dislodges the stomach a fraction or two as we attempt to disentangle our extremity from the elastic nothingness that now clings to it like etherous mire. Fretting and fidgeting for a while, we finally manage to liberate it, and hurriedly we rescind our step. We should never, etc. Out of immediate danger now, we quickly straighten the tenuous stem of our spine and rock ourselves motionless (a movement interchangeable with glasses put down in a huff). There. Time to catch our breath. Time to reconsider.

For example: the floor we are on. Odd, is it not?, what with those five or six doors shoulder to shoulder in such mishap fashion (as if assembled by a one-handed stage director when both drunk and dejected). Let us try them, though, despite their shameless prevarication, as they might still reveal something. After having knocked on a couple, we find one door that soundlessly glides open on first contact with our knuckle. Stepping inside, we search skittishly but conscientiously through the apartment's rooms. Nothing remarkable, however. Heavy furniture covered with dust, stacks of old newspapers, a refrigerator (defrosted), assorted pieces of china—that sort of thing. On a wall a picture of what seems to be a pair of siblings, on another a still of what looks like a commemorative tablet. The soothing calm of the latter is especially enticing to our mind. When we step closer, we notice that the picture contains a whitish inscription flittering across a slate of something or another placed on a heap of granular dust. The still is of the oddly mesmerizing kind that, given the proper hypomnemic circumstances, we might remain standing there, trailing those fumescent wafts until fusing with them. But instead, pulling the apathetic curtain from one of the windows, we sober up and steal a view of the fire wall across the street. (A dull spasm of recognition crumbles our belly like a sheet of paper.) Then, finally, we retrace our steps to the stairway. Apparently, nobody has lived here for a long time. The air has turned stale and sawdusty. No point in staying.

Although we seem to know what we are doing, as we ponder our next movements, we realize we are aware merely of the outline of their objective—yet like all voids, our curiosity, now a sizable entity of its own, craves to be sated. After having ransacked three or four other lodgings, we thus arrive at a door in the confusing interior of an apartment that, upon crossing its threshold, immediately gives us that thick, tangy feeling of foreboding. What a biscuity smell. Pushing down the handle, we hold our breath. No such luck: it creaks a bit, but does not budge. As we bend down to inspect the lock, for a second and a half, we imagine that we will be able to look inside and make out the corner of a mattress, say, a chair and an ashtray, perhaps also some strange little figurine (tin soldier?) on what will turn out to be a table. But alas, as we are level with the lock, we notice a key inserted from the other side. Faint light is caught in the hermetic clutter of metals, but that is all. Next we look to see whether the slim slot under the door might accommodate an insinuating sheet of paper on which we may inveigle the key to fall and be drawn out to our expectant hand. When we discover a threshold, however, we are forced to abandon the idea. Thus we examine the hinges in the hope that it might be possible to unhook the door, but, of course, it is attached on the inside. When we figure out, finally, the degree of brutal strength required to force an entry—and abandon that idea, too—we are compelled to leave the room to its mysterious fate, now entirely convinced that what we sought, whatever it was, in fact was there. If only—but no.

On our downy way downstairs again (the eyes have now become used to the dark, and, once more, our feet feel secure), we see two open windows out of which some emaciated light, sliced horizontally, emerges through drawn blinds. Stray radiance, it flickers with butterflyish indecision. Perhaps it is emanating from a couple of candles about to reach their bantam base. For a moment we believe that this must be the room we just attempted to enter, but as we move on we realize that the other one was located on the second floor whereas this one is on the first. The thought of a secret passage linking the two is abandoned as being possible only in drugged or draughty minds. Still, we cannot entirely shed the suspicion that the two are connected, and this brief bump of prescience on our route downstairs—based on thin air and nonsense—is sufficient to ensure that we, redoubtable explorers, shall bring back the feeling that there was, well, *quelque chose*. Like the astrologer who connects two stars as part of one constellation, henceforth we shall live with the perception of a living link between accidental occurrences. That this juncture is less trustworthy than a chord of fog does not bother us in the least. We ourselves are the connective, regardless of how *grisant* it might be.

Arriving on the ground floor a few moments later, having tightened the collar of our greatcoat against the bad weather—rain has started to fall heavy as abandoned hearts—we observe with curiosity, on the other side of the courtyard, two, it seems, dunly dressed ambulance workers place an old man on a stretcher (cane—is it not?—on top), preparing to carry him upstairs, when suddenly they become aware of the squeakeous sound emancipating itself from the back door we are just opening. Perturbed, we shake our head like wet lettuce, withdrawing faster than shades at noon. For some reason, we are afraid of being seen. Instead, we walk briskly through the outer hall, but at the very moment we are about to pass through the front door into Silence and Unconcern—the adventure we thought was ending turns out merely to have started—a strange creature disengages itself from the feathered armpit of dusk, like a hindsight almost, and stares at us with eyes as unpleasant as gulps of cold water. Hardly human, nor, however, entirely beast.

Naturally, we expect a sardonic comment or some insinuating suggestion, soft and menacing as a pimp's whisper, but instead the creature merely laughs like rattling leaves or squeaking shoe soles. Having gotten a hold of ourselves, we open our arms in feigned amazement—much in the manner, in fact, of the lady whom we cannot see on the other side of the door, but who simultaneously distends her umbrella after having lost something on the ground—and we summon the courage to ask whom we have the honor of meeting. "Drdk" comes the crumpled answer; wind and rain pilfer the rest. Now, now, how might we possibly retrieve the name from syllabic air so quickly dispersed? Although we were all ears, we fail to recover it, but we are fairly certain we caught at least a sliver of Slavonic or German dialect. Was it *Dreck*, perhaps? Writing off further efforts as hopeless, we nod our head instead in meaningless approval, realizing that the only part of the name likely to remain logged in our memory is its slag. Almost dregs, we think. Perhaps fitting for such a forlorn creature.

That we manage to put into shape these toilsome thoughts during a moment as brief as that of a train rushing past a crossing is due to the bars of representation: being lowered, they offer us an interlude in which to stretch the loins of conjecture. During this suitable break our eyes also have the opportunity to scrutinize more closely the creature in front of them. At first sight it looked like a star-shaped spool and appeared, we also noticed, to be dressed in a simple knit made of variegated threads (yellow dominating). But now we realize not only that it looks like a stranger sort of a six-sided bobbin, bunched up as if resisting growth, but also that a small black rod protrudes from under its star-shaped middle (where the yellow is concentrated) on which it seems to balance. Perhaps it has only one leg, we feebly manage to reflect (what curious predicament, in that case), but then our thoughts—

or faded facsimiles thereof—are mercifully interrupted. Distant bells are suddenly doing their rapping best at chiming, then the bars are being lifted with that tick-tack-tingling precision. No room for further reflection, i.e.

As if another dimension again laid claim to it, our stranger appears nervous and agitated by the sound. Probably it would prove futile, we reason as the creature presently wriggle-waddles away with an ashen coordination to its movements, to imagine that it once might have acted like a normal, animated noun. At least no attributes suggested as much. It seemed more like a batch of stray properties, really, daubed with a recondite gloss. But on the other hand, nowhere were we able to discern scars or seams that might have indicated that we had encountered, as it were, an adjectival agglomeration or a compound verb (also known as homunculi and golems, respectively). The creature most certainly did not correspond to anything we have seen in real life or read about in school, yet it still struck us as being as single-minded as a human. There is no point in stating anything more specific, though, except perhaps to say that it also appeared to be quite mobile and most likely would not allow itself to be caught that easily. "Where do you live?," we finally shout in the direction of the bent back now fading into a wild, plumbeous dusk the way a drawer disappears into its desk. "No fixed abode," we hear the answer bounce off the violaceous humidity that soaks the scene like so much ink, to be followed immediately by a trickle of rattling laughter discharged as if it had been stuck for too long in a place without lungs. (A squeaking sound, like wood rubbing on wood.)

Are we any wiser? Hardly. The creature has vanished as willingly as an object dropped in water. Alone again, we ransack our memory to determine what happened. (Personally we might prefer to ease, no, to erase, ourselves into disappearance, for example by turning through the door here and out into the street—in which case, further away, we would notice a white back sheltered under a neat umbrella against the darkening rain now pouring down like so many dogged crazes. But of course we stop short of this clueless desire, as any nonsensical waft of wind would be counted on to fill

the vacuum left behind, rearranging our hardwon designs into dust and disbelief. Instead we ask:) Was it an accident? Surely not. Was it fate? Perhaps. Was it, ah, a matter of fact? In its own manner: of course. The bundle of properties we encountered may have been knocked together out of stuff that was literally untrue, but it remains metaphorically apt. So? So perhaps this is the way the world looks before it has been formed into solid, stultifying matter, brought about by hands more nimble and numerous than ours. If you say so; it is possible. But let us not leave out oblivion, in that case. Oblivion? Yes, after all, that is what we are getting at, is it not? Is it? Well, oblivion or whatever exists before memory does . . . that tiny heap of dust . . . that pile of sheddings . . . and here it comes, anyway, no point in ignoring it . . . Wait. Hold. Before it arrives, please, a last word about the funereal collection of which we thus would seem to be speaking, erected where a brass sharpener does its recurrent, no, by now its pleonastic duty. (We are quoting from memory, paraphrasing a recollection.) What of it? Well, if it is the scattered maze of moments and shadows of movements in which forgetting is gathered . . . . Yes? . . . then if it is now coming . . . . Yes? . . . it must be returning to scratch, must it not? Huh? That is: coming full cycle? That is: to a close? Why, yes, conceivably. That does seem to be the case. Like a train of thought chewing its own rear. Form finally becoming content. That sort of thing. Well, then, consider those jagged sheddings of squandered action. All right. Are they not the flakes and flukes providing the matter of our story? Come again? The flakes and flukes. Providing the matter. Of our story. But of course. So that livid litter . . . there, over there . . . demarcates both a point of departure and a point of return? Yes. Does such nulliverse not— — — — — —
— — — — — — — — — — — — — — — — — —
— — — — — — — — — — — — — — — — — —
— — — — — — — — — — — — — — — — — —
— — — — — — — — — — — — — — — — — —
— — — — — — — — — — — — — — — — — —
— — — — — — — — — — — — — — — — — —

―― ―― ―― ―― ―― ―― ―― ―― ―― ―― ―― ―― ―― ―― ――
―― ―― ―― ―― ―― ―― ―― ―― ―― ―― ―― ―― ―― ―― ――
―― ―― ―― ―― ―― ―― ―― ―― ―― ―― ―― ―― ―― ―― ――
―― ―― ―― ―― ―― ―― ―― ―― ―― ―― ―― ―― ―― ―― ――
―― ―― ―― ―― ―― ―― ―― as drowsy clouds drifting by, shaking their woolly heads like a dotard who, standing in front of an unreliable mirror, no longer remembers what he wished to recall (hands trembling with useless abandon), while a little boy, having left his homework and two friends, assuming he had been sitting at his feet, would have thought he witnessed a magician in the process of conjuring forth an unexpected creature or forlorn thing, transparent as cellophane yet solid enough to be visualized in that chancy, lickety-split way of sightings, and suddenly the old man stands up, thwarted by what ought to come but, of course, does not, and thereafter, shaking his shoulders in profitless dismay, he sort-of-meets the look of the non-existing child, uninhabited eyes not seeing staring eyes, and soundlessly shapes a slew of saliva-lined stutterings with his immaterial mouth of which merely the lips' disembodied orb now remain. O-O-O. Agape and suspended, as if his oral office had been broken into. There is a buttoned-up noise, spilled out like coffee grounds, but then only breathing as heavy as rejected proposals.

Forgetting, we say, apparently not entirely oblivious, but what do we know about forgetting? Oblivion, we reassert, and believe that we thereby can pin down whatever the word allegedly contains. But forgetting is neither in a pinpoint nor in down, but merely consists of lithe loss and the avowal of diffusion—as in the gradual decomposition of a purpose, for example, an action we might analogize to the leisurely dispersal of pencil dust, that villainous disintegration enacted by a blithe brass sharpener with such dutiful wantonness; or in the ten times ten thousand bricks of a crumbling wall happy to trade places, finally, with emptiness; or in as many leaves scooped up with choice rapture into a fistful of wind; or in any striated scatter of the white seeds of winter (a vague chill of restlessness clinging to the motion); or in the studious slip of sand sliding into the has-been-well of an hourglass, one businesslike grain after the other; or in stones skidding across lethal water before maturity catches up with their momentum, forcing them to accept their fate with a brief bend of neck as they sink in an angle that, first, pushes an admirable twenty degrees, but soon thereafter folds into virtuous verticality; or in accidentally spilled beans that are swept up with brisk broom and drowsy dustpan to be thrown, with a handcuffed twist, into the sturdy fellow of a waste basket well placed under a regurgitating sink (where the wedding rice left untouched by pigeons now is swelling in humdrum fashion thanks to the last globs of milk emitted by a resentful carton); or in any immensity able to claim the vastness of oceans and fire walls—or, for that matter, of a keyboard's forty or so tenderly cupped squares; or in ashes negotiating their thinning prospects in a tray of tin; or in spider web as inkily latticed as wetlooking stockings (gleaming shins, whispering calves); or in the wrinkles produced in a palm closing; or in whirling whirling palettes; or in a thousand worries and as many years; or in pockets full of pebbles; or in dungeons dense with dragons' teeth; or in eyes filled to the brim by blankness; or in trees full of birds, birds full of worms, worms full of rice; or in other worms, having eloped, now furtively making it into an oblong casket soon to be placed in an altogether unusual mausoleum never to be seen again; or in the unruly relish of decay, decay, decay; or in nonsensical nights spent in the spells and folds of autonomous dreams; or in forgotten shadows left hanging on nails in unopened closets; or in the teasy wafts of suspicion, trying to trail in a manner to seem both transparent and opportune; or, again, in decay; or in the surreptitious commerce of saliva, stones, and silence, transacted in a mouth finally put to prudent purpose; or in expectations as wobbly as a pneumatically-challenged dove's attempt to bypass the laws of gravity; or in soil, spoil, and discharges, in crap, clay, muck, and mire, in filth and refuse, in dregs, dung, and the easings of nature; but also in moist manure and teeming compost, and in gravel as elusive as the tiny crepitations of consonantic discomfort studding the primadonna's otherwise rapturous release of ardor; or in scraped-off wood and scales, for that matter (listen to their wiry and swift, sated silence), and in flakes and fluff flourishing as colds in a nursery; or in the dangerous game of fingers five and fumbling; or in interruptions; or in fatigue, that endless, reckless, longed-for exhaustion, so sweetly heedless, when it arrives, that limbs abandon their business in a lazy clamor of confused delight: so, then, to let go, too, to relax and to relinquish; to lose the thread and to slip up; to be defeated, interrupted, and terminated; to lay off and to leave in; to discontinue and to be done for, to be taken out of context, then shaken out of shape (a windful of unnerving loss); to disregard, set aside, and overlook; to efface, neglect, and omit; to become weary and to turn tired; to give in and to fade out, to abandon, but also to forget; yes, to forget; with relish, joy, and predilection, decidedly and irrevocably, utterly and wholeheartedly, definitely at long last incontrovertibly, endlessly finally and eternally, at least now and at least here, at last unendingly and unerringly, so that then and there and here and now it is all here and now, at least at last and for ever after; and thus to forget the forgetting; and to forget the forgetting of the forgotten; and to forget these words, too, consigned to so much gimcrack fretting . . . so that all that remains, in the end, is merely a hissing heap of haze—shade, sound, and shape, in short—nothing more, really, and we dream ourselves into the voidful depth of a mirror shimmering in its shiny coat of unconcern . . . bubbles breaking, dread disintegrating, silken shelter shed and shun . . . now metamogrifying instead, with wondrous consequences, into something else . . . something like . . . loss. Yes. Pure and pernicious l o s s. That wide, wild world of dispersal, glimpsed as if through fingers fighting fright. Oh, all to end.

And then it happens. The gray that has surrounded us with such quiescent abandon seems to flatten all remaining depth into surface, volume into veneer, so that the only things still to be grasped are figures and hues continually shifting within a solitary plane of perspective. ("It is a queer enterprise," *Ada* notes, "this attempt to determine the nature of something consisting of phantomatic phases.") We stir a while to see if our fluttering movement might produce, when observed closely, an aperture, but everything is so even and smooth that, had our motions been words, every one would have petered out with the dull indistinction of a dactyl. What if this nullity, now collapsed, it seems, like a Japanese rice-paper lamp, is that ovoid vesicle out of which our gray region once was formed? A kind of deflated universe, as it were, or nulliverse, now all immobility and projection? And what if its monodimensional jumble—surrounding us like boxes and furniture randomly put down by the lubberly movers of sleep—what if it corresponds, after all, to the "hazy, rubbery" receptacle we have courted with such crazy infatuation?

Could it be? In order to clarify these questions we would need a stick as well as the possibility of using it. Also, we would need a bundle of future and conditional clauses, which we could launch ahead of us like orphaned arrows to determine, if possible (but then only from the sound), whether what flattens this circumscribed world is that old, tattered emptiness or a novel form of etherous scandal. Suspended in sensuous seeing, however, housed within a thin foil of fluctuation, we cannot tell. All we perceive as we continue to stare into the silvery opaqueness, writhing slightly because unsupervised, is a smudgy, circular movement with something hovering in its middle, a tiny *quelque chose* cramped as into a cylinder, emitting a faint flicker of almost violaceous light. It looks like an eye, does it not?, made of sapphire perhaps, returning our zeroish stare with benevolent indifference. We could fall into this depthless well, we realize, as easily as into the abyssal abode of a pupil, stickily exhaling, stickily inhaling an entire universe through its flat, bobbing aperture. A window of opportunity? Hardly. One twinkle and it would all be out. What a *pointe assassine*.

Are we even "comparatively"? Aquamarine darkness is suddenly streaming into our flat, fidgety space, like water through a leak in a wafer-thin vessel. We can tell this is the end, however poorly represented. There is nothing to latch on to. We are losing both sight and string. Straws are of no avail—least of all that crumbling one that, we notice, is now in the none too delicate process of disentagling itself from our spasmodic digits in order to slowly, unassumingly, put itself to horizontal rest somewhere above us, a neutral brow above a dimming eye. What an epitaph. Just that even, yellow line—like a cardiogram gone flat. No longer vying for inclusion in the reality so fuzzily glanced below. And what of *it*? Hard to glance, harder to gloss. As it dissolves to wistfulness, sight turns into sigh, and further reports would be mere accretions of trepidation, behaving (however rightly) as if their true meaning resided elsewhere—nonsensical wafts of *fioriture*, that is, no more, vainly trying to keep on the surface the way chalk does on a board, only to be wiped out by a palmful of forgetting. We said so: a cloud of unknowing. So *this* is what it was for? Our mouth's mutinous labor? Now immobilized by the inexistent design, that hapless shape, hovering a while as a harangue in memory's humming space, then tenderly faced and effaced (etherous lunulae gravesheeting half-vivid, half-livid nothing)? Oh, it will be cold getting out of this indigo element.

As the straw slips out of grasp, our eyes close like a drawer returned to its dejected desk, and left is only the orphaned thought, trailing *in vacuo*, whether being without being is not, after all, blue.

Acknowledgments

Not so much a translation as a version—rewritten in English—of the original Swedish, *The Gray Book* would not have become legible without the help of Jenny Jochens. A gray eminence indeed, her support has been unwavering from the first syllable mouthed to the last period put.

Although, to my knowledge, very little has been written on grayness in literature, there are a handful of studies that have provided me with inspiration, among them books by Henry Petroski and Brian Rotman—on the history of the pencil and the semiotics of zero, respectively. I should also like to mention two essays by Werner Hamacher: one on tears, the other on clouds.

But the shadow cast most conspicuously across the pages of this book belongs, of course, to the author of that lithe and lovely treatise entitled *On Being Blue*. It is only proper that the patch of prose contained within the present covers be dedicated to him.

MERIDIAN

Crossing Aesthetics

Aris Fioretos, *The Gray Book*

Deborah Esch, *In the Event: Reading Journalism, Reading Theory*

Winfried Menninghaus, *In Praise of Nonsense: Kant and Bluebeard*

Giorgio Agamben, *The Man Without Content*

Giorgio Agamben, *The End of the Poem: Essays in Poetics*

Theodor W. Adorno, *Sound Figures*

Louis Marin, *Sublime Poussin*

Philippe Lacoue-Labarthe, *Poetry as Experience*

Jacques Derrida, *Resistances of Psychoanalysis*

Marc Froment-Meurice, *That Is to Say: Heidegger's Poetics*

Francis Ponge, *Soap*

Philippe Lacoue-Labarthe, *Typography: Mimesis, Philosophy, Politics*

Giorgio Agamben, *Homo Sacer: Sovereign Power and Bare Life*

Emmanuel Levinas, *Of God Who Comes to Mind*

Bernard Stiegler, *Technics and Time, 1: The Fault of Epimetheus*

Werner Hamacher, *pleroma—Reading in Hegel*

Serge Leclaire, *Psychoanalyzing: On the Order of the Unconscious and the Practice of the Letter*

Serge Leclaire, *A Child Is Being Killed: On Primary Narcissism and the Death Drive*

Sigmund Freud, *Writings on Art and Literature*

Cornelius Castoriadis, *World in Fragments: Writings on Politics, Society, Psychoanalysis, and the Imagination*

Thomas Keenan, *Fables of Responsibility: Aberrations and Predicaments in Ethics and Politics*

Emmanuel Levinas, *Proper Names*

Alexander García Düttmann, *At Odds with AIDS: Thinking and Talking About a Virus*

Maurice Blanchot, *Friendship*

Jean-Luc Nancy, *The Muses*

Massimo Cacciari, *Posthumous People: Vienna at the Turning Point*

David E. Wellbery, *The Specular Moment: Goethe's Early Lyric and the Beginnings of Romanticism*

Edmond Jabès, *The Little Book of Unsuspected Subversion*

Hans-Jost Frey, *Studies in Poetic Discourse: Mallarmé, Baudelaire, Rimbaud, Hölderlin*

Pierre Bourdieu, *The Rules of Art: Genesis and Structure of the Literary Field*

Nicolas Abraham, *Rhythms: On the Work, Translation, and Psychoanalysis*

Jacques Derrida, *On the Name*

David Wills, *Prosthesis*

Maurice Blanchot, *The Work of Fire*

Jacques Derrida, *Points . . . : Interviews, 1974–1994*

J. Hillis Miller, *Topographies*

Philippe Lacoue-Labarthe, *Musica Ficta (Figures of Wagner)*

Jacques Derrida, *Aporias*

Emmanuel Levinas, *Outside the Subject*

Jean-François Lyotard, *Lessons on the Analytic of the Sublime*

Peter Fenves, *"Chatter": Language and History in Kierkegaard*

Jean-Luc Nancy, *The Experience of Freedom*

Jean-Joseph Goux, *Oedipus, Philosopher*

Haun Saussy, *The Problem of a Chinese Aesthetic*

Jean-Luc Nancy, *The Birth to Presence*

Library of Congress Cataloging-in-Publication Data

Fioretos, Aris.
   [Den grå boken. English]
   The Gray book / Aris Fioretos.
   p. cm. — (Meridian, crossing aesthetics)
   ISBN 0-8047-3537-9 (cloth). — ISBN 0-8047-3538-7 (paper)
   1. Aesthetics, Modern.   I. Title.   II. Series: Meridian (Stanford, Calif.)
BH151.F49   1999
839.74'74—dc21   98-47075

∞ This book is printed on acid-free, recycled paper.

Original printing 1999
Last figure below indicates year of this printing:
08   07   06   05   04   03   02   01   00   99

The authorized representative in the EU for product safety and compliance is:
Mare Nostrum Group
B.V Doelen 72
4831 GR Breda
The Netherlands

www.ingramcontent.com/pod-product-compliance
Lightning Source LLC
Chambersburg PA
CBHW021735220426
43662CB00008B/865